MORE BRAIN SCRAPS

Pendra J. King

I dedicate this book to the one who has always deserved my love.

CONTENTS

FOREWORD

Last year when I started pulling Brain Scraps together, I was hoping a few generous friends would buy my book and enjoy it. As one who writes for fun and self satisfaction, my only goal is to entertain you, the reader. After receiving messages, texts, phone calls, and handwritten letters asking for another round of Brain Scraps, I decided to give it a go. I've been thumbing through my notebooks to find a good mix of stories to delight you. In this volume you'll find more family stories, a few gems from some beloved senior citizens, and several ramblings from my beanie little noggin. Grab your favorite coffee mug and settle in for a bit.

Enjoy!

WRITTEN IN STONE

One of my mother's favorite sayings to us when we were little was, "Put it away NEATLY where it belongs!" It could be the folded laundry, toys, dishes, or whatever was not in its proper place. Over and over again, we'd hear those words. Put it away NEATLY where it belongs. When you hear something on a regular basis, it becomes a habit, and that's what Mickey was hoping to instill in all of us. Our home wasn't going to be in any magazine spread, but Mickey really did try to keep it somewhat presentable. With six kids underfoot, I can only imagine how impossible that task must have seemed on most days.

Fast forward to many years later. One of my sisters and I were visiting our parents on a bright Sunday morning. We sat around the kitchen table reading the Sunday paper, eating doughnuts, and shooting the breeze. We were catching up on each other's lives, and what was going on in the world. We started talking about favorite expressions the folks had and my sister and I started imitating our parents. I lowered my voice and, in my best Oscar voice, stated, "Won't take but ten minutes." That was one of our father's favorite expressions when he told us to do a chore. It NEVER took only ten minutes. Doing dishes or mowing the grass was always at least an hour-long chore. No task ever took ten minutes in a family of eight.

We all laughed at my Oscar impression, then my sister chimed in with her own. "Life is rarely fair," which was another one of my mother's favorites.

I popped up with, "Everything happens for a reason," rolling my eyes because we rarely get to know the reason why bad things happen in our lives.

My sister squared her shoulders to do her Ma imitation and clearly intoned, "Put it away NEATLY where it belongs!" We all lost it. She was spot-on. My parents took all of this in good stride and were actually happy that we'd been paying attention all those years. Jokingly, my sister said, "Ma, when you die, we're going to put that on your tombstone. Here lies Ma, neatly, where she belongs!"

And that's how it came to be. My mother LOVED that idea. My father nodded eagerly. It was perfect. Not long after that humorous conversation at the kitchen table, my brother Tyler was killed at the tender age of 26. My folks aged 50 years overnight. They were faced with the daunting task of buying his burial plot and headstone. They had enough foresight to buy their own plot and stone at the same time so the surviving children wouldn't have to make any decisions when the time came for them to be planted. When my parents ordered their stone, they gave the engraver their birthdates, their marriage date, and then on the base of the stone was my mother's request: Here lies Ma, neatly, where she belongs.

Every time my mother would visit Tyler's grave, she'd look over at her stone in the next plot and start to laugh. I even have pictures of her lying on top of where she'd eventually be laid to rest, with her head resting near the stone. I have a picture of her on her elbows and knees with her butt in the air so people could kiss her ass good-bye. What a sense of humor. In a way it was comforting to know she had a spot waiting for her next to her son. She prayed she'd never have to buy another burial spot for any of her other children, and her wish was granted. Mickey died in 2002 and was placed exactly where she wanted.

******

A little side note here: When my brother was buried in 1985, the funeral director had positioned my brother's casket with the foot of it facing where the headstone would eventually be placed. My mother spoke up and politely pointed out the mistake. The funeral director quietly explained the casket was placed in that position deliberately. It was for when the resurrection happened. Most Christians tend to bury their dead facing the east. This is because they believe in the second coming of Christ and scripture teaches that he will come from the east. In this manner, they place their dead in a position so they can meet Christ face-to-face during his second coming.

NO, that was NOT how it was going to be with her son's grave. She insisted the casket be turned around so his head was where his headstone would be. Being the considerate man he was, he promptly had his crew carefully turn Tyler's casket so the head was in the opposite direction. My mother didn't believe in bodies flying out of the ground on any certain day. In her heart she believed his spirit had already left his earthbound body. That night, Ma made all of us swear that she'd be placed the same way, her head at her headstone, not backward. We all gave our solemn promise we'd make sure she was placed correctly. Sure enough, that day came in October of 2002. We gathered around the tarp-covered pile of dirt next to the open hole over which my mother's box hovered. As the last words were said, I looked at each of my siblings and my father. We were all looking at the casket and making sure the head was in the proper location. A short giggle was heard. Then a small snort. Our eyes darted back and forth from the headstone to each other's faces. With the final words said, we headed back to our cars and left the cemetery, leaving Ma to rest, neatly, where she belongs.

AT THE AUCTION

"There's a farm dispersal near Malone tomorrow. Who wants to go?" Oscar casually tossed the invitation out to us kids while we were all sitting around the dinner table one night.

"No thanks! I see enough of those long-faced whores every morning and night! Why would I want to go watch you buy some more?" My brother Tyler always called the cows long-faced whores. For some reason that got a chuckle out of our folks.

My sister didn't even acknowledge the invitation. She barely knew where the barn was, let alone have an interest in going to a farm auction.

That left just my younger brother and me. We looked at each other with that knowing grin on our faces.

"I WANNA GO!" Tim chirped.

"ME TOO!" was my input.

And there it was. The next day three of us were headed for an auction.

We kids had been to enough auctions with our father to know the rules. When Oscar went to a sale, he was on a mission. His attention was on the cattle and equipment. He didn't have the time or patience to chase after wayward children, even if they did come from his own loins. I'm sure he wouldn't have minded leaving a few of us at the sales now and then, but he knew our mother probably wouldn't have approved of his actions, so he always made sure to arrive home with the same number of kids he took. Rule number one: don't stray.

If it was a farm auction, the equipment for sale was usually lined up outside where buyers could inspect the pieces before they bid. Everything sold "as is" and all sales were final. The cattle would be inside, or at least in open pens where potential buyers could get a good look at the animals. Oscar would take his time and first check out any machinery he might want or need, then move on to the cows. Now here's the thing about going to an auction with Oscar: people knew Oscar was an excellent herdsman. They also knew he was good at getting bargains. Sometimes a few people would spot Oscar and follow him around in a subtle, casual way. I admit Oscar wasn't perfect, but his judgment was usually spot-on and very well trusted. If they saw Oscar eyeing a piece of equipment or certain cows, they'd make note of it. The chance to snag a cow that Oscar King had been eyeballing was a feather in anyone's cap. Little did they know what he was really doing. Rule two was a good one: keep your eye on people watching Oscar. Oh, this was fun because we felt like we were spying on the spies. He was flattered and his ego was boosted every time he went to a sale and saw a few other guys watching him as he strolled through the lineup. He'd worked hard all his life to learn the ins and outs of cattle, and it showed.

Once in a while if there was a particular piece of machinery Oscar really needed, he'd look it over and say to us kids (in a loud enough voice for others to overhear), "Yeah, this plow would be okay if it didn't have those tiny cracks down there. Looks like it'll need some welding. Probably gonna break the first time around the field." There weren't any little cracks in that plow, but it sure scared off any other potential buyer. He'd do that with almost any piece of machinery he desperately needed. Nine times out of ten, he'd be the only bidder or he'd win the bid quickly because the other person would back down thinking about repairs. When it came to the cows, he'd walk through once giving just a cursory glance, then he'd go back through again and play the game. He'd stop at some not too awful cows and nod, check out udders, make notes in his sale booklet, then move along. He'd always pick cows that were about a 5 on a scale of 1 to 10. The guys watching him would think,

"Damn, he must see something we don't. Put a check mark next to that one's number." Oscar was highly skilled at summing up a cow's worth with just a few quick glances. He was never obvious when he was checking out an animal he really wanted. He'd make a fuss over the one standing *next* to his herd's next addition, but never gave the best ones any direct attention. This threw the other farmers off and he knew it. All's fair in love and war and cattle auctions!

Rule number three was to never, EVER, under any circumstances wave at a friend, scratch your ear, or shoo a fly in front of your face. We were pretty sure no auctioneer would take a child's movement as an actual bid but, hey, you never know. No sense taking a chance of winning a bid on a ten-year-old dry jersey cow. Oscar knew all the local auctioneers and made a point of going over to whomever was conducting the sale to shake his hand. He was always up front with the auctioneers and let them know he was there to buy, so keep an eye on him. And then the fun started. Whether it was the machinery or the cattle, Oscar knew exactly what he was willing to pay. He'd sit in a spot with a direct line of sight to the auctioneer.

"WHO'LL GIMME TWO HUNNER-TWO HUNNER NOW THREE! THREE-HUNNER THREE-HUNNER- HUNNER THERE'S THREE NOW FOUR THERE'S FOUR!" the auctioneer would rattle quickly in his rolling lingo. Hands would go up, hands would go down. Frustrated bidders would snap their necks at the person outbidding them. This is an arena where men fought to the death. (Death of their checkbooks, that is.) "I GOT FOUR HUNNER GOING ONCE, TWICE, SOLD! TO MR. SMITH FOR FOUR HUNDRED DOLLARS!"

"NEXT UP IS COW NUMBER 22. WHO'LL START ME WITH FIVE HUNNER FIVE HUNNER ANYONE FI-HUNNER?" the microphone blared. Nobody's hand went up. "WE GOT FIVE HUNNER NOW SIX! SIX HUNNER ANYONE GIMME SIX SIX SIX?" People looked around. Still no hands. Who the hell had bid five hundred? Maybe the auctioneer had imagined a bid? No, he couldn't do that. Some guy then timidly held up his hand and the auctioneer pointed at him and hollered, "I SEE SIX! WE GOT SIX HUNNER NOW DO I HEAR SEVEN? C'MON GIMME GIMME SEVEN SEVEN HUNNER! WHO'S GONNA GIMME . . . THERE WE GOT SEVEN HUNNER NOW!"

The heads started turning, looking left, looking right. Puzzled faces glanced at the auctioneer then back to the lone bidder with a confused look on his face.

"WE GOT SEVEN SEVEN SEVEN, NOW WHO'LL GIMME EIGHT?" By this time everybody was confused, especially that one guy who appeared to be bidding alone, but the price of that damned cow kept going up. Finally, the auctioneer's voice came out with, "I GOT SEVEN SEVEN SEVEN! LAST CALL! GOING ONCE, GOING TWICE, SOLD! TO OSCAR KING FOR SEVEN HUNDRED DOLLARS!"

All heads turned. Oscar's hand hadn't gone up once. No auction paddle with a number on it. No hand waving. No hat in the air. No hollered yelp. What the hell was going on? People were scratching their heads. A few more cows went by and were auctioned off without incident.

Then another choice Holstein showed up. "I'M GONNA START THIS ONE WITH SIX HUNNER, SIX HUNNER THERE'S SIX! NOW WHO'LL GIMME GIMME GIMME SEVEN?" Nobody saw a hand go up for that six-hundred-dollar bid. Could it have been Oscar? Nobody saw him do anything. Someone bid seven hundred. "THERE'S A SEVEN HUNNER, SEVEN! NOW WHO WANTS HER FOR EIGHT? EIGHT? EIGHT? NOW WE GOT EIGHT. NINE? HERE WE GO HERE WE GO GOIN' FOR NINE WHO WANTS HER FOR NINE?" Another hand shot up. "NOW NINE AND TEN? ONE THOUSAND WHO'LL GIMME TEN FOR HER? THERE WE ARE, TEN!"

Oscar's hands were firmly in his lap. This wasn't a cow he'd been eyeballing, so it couldn't have been Oscar who had bid on it. His hands aren't THAT fast to go up and down before anyone could see him. "GOING ONCE, GOING TWICE, SOLD! TO OSCAR KING FOR ONE THOUSAND DOLLARS! NEXT UP IS . . ."

Now that Oscar is gone and there are no more auctions to

be had, I'll tell you how he did it. Oscar's trademark was his cigar. For most of his farming career he smoked cigars. When he went to the auctions, he made sure to say hello to the auctioneers and, if there happened to be a new guy in charge, he'd quietly let him know to watch for his cigar. If he flipped it up and down, that meant yes, that was his bid. If the bid was back to him and he didn't want it, he'd move the cigar back and forth sideways. Just very small movements, but enough so the auctioneer could see it. This was fun for Oscar and it added a bit of mystery and hype for the auctioneers too. They loved it. People would "jokingly" ask Oscar if he had some sort of mental telepathy with the auctioneers. He'd just laugh and say, "Of course! Doesn't everybody?"

I've been to numerous auctions since Oscar's death in 2013, but they just aren't the same anymore. Holding a paddle with a number on it or raising my hand to bid on that box of books seems so boring and ordinary. Now and then if I pay close attention, I swear I can smell a faint whiff of cigar smoke.

LICENSE AND REGISTRATION, PLEASE

I'm a sucker for a good love story. I used to watch those sappy Hallmark movies until I realized every single one of them was the same, they just changed the name of the town and what the main character was driving for a vehicle. Still, the thought of love winning out every time was heartwarming. What a mush!

In July 2019, I was driving back from my camp in New Hampshire. (More on that another time. That's a whole chapter in itself.) It was raining. Hard. A torrential downpour is how I'd best describe the precipitation that particular day. Even with my windshield wipers going as fast as they could, they didn't keep up with the amount of water pouring from the heavens. I could have been driving neck-deep in a riverbed for all I knew. Visibility was zilch. Zero. I knew it was only a matter of time before I rear-ended someone or maybe I'd get t-boned. *This is stupid*, I thought. *Just pull over and wait it out. I'm retired, I don't have to be home at any certain time, and I do want to arrive alive.* All logical thoughts, so I inched my way into the closest town, which was Morrisville, Vermont. I found a McDonald's and pulled in, killed the motor, and tippy-toe trotted inside. Only two people were at the counter ordering their meals, and four tables were taken in the main dining area. Plenty of room for one more soaked patron. I moseyed up to the counter and placed my order. Every now and then out of respect for Kinsey Millhone I'll order a quarter pounder with cheese, so I did just that and a large cup of coffee. After a couple of minutes my order was filled so I hoisted my tray and headed to the tables.

At one table sat a pair of teenage girls showing each other who knows what on their phones, giggling every three seconds as gasps of OH-MY-GAWD! escaped their mouths. Surely they didn't need an old lady sitting next to them as they drooled over the Biebs or Harry. I looked to my left and there was an older couple sitting side by side on a bench seat. The table next to them was empty and clean. That was my target. I sat down and surveyed the rest of the small dining area. Besides the two girls and the older couple, there was a father and son duo seated near the window. The lad was about four years old, and he was lining up his french fries then eating them one by one. His father beamed with pride. I guessed dad was either an accountant or an engineer. The only other occupied table was near the bathroom and a rather frazzled looking woman was sitting there with her laptop, cell phone, and calculator. Upon further inspection, I deduced she was the manager and was either tallying up sales or ordering more Big Mac fixins.

I carefully unwrapped my QPW/C to make sure none of the cheese stuck to the paper. I flipped the lid off my coffee because, although I wasn't in a big hurry, I did want to drink the coffee sometime that afternoon, preferably with my burger. Just as I sunk my teeth into the beef, I heard the older woman next to me say, "Sixty. Sixty years! Where did the time go?"

My ears pricked up a bit. I've turned eavesdropping into an art. Strike that . . . I've sharpened my enhanced listening skills for my own amusement and possibly yours. (That sounds nicer, doesn't it?)

"I don't know where it went, but I do know it went fast!" The gentleman's face crinkled up as he gave her a smile. I was watching out of the corner of my eye, but still getting the full picture.

I set my burger down, took an anticipatory sip of the lava

java in my cup, and nonchalantly looked over at the couple to my right. "Excuse me. I couldn't help but overhear you. Did you say sixty years? As in you've been together for sixty years?" The crepe-skinned woman turned her head at me and smiled. Her husband leaned forward a little so he could see around her and said to me, "Yes ma'am! We've been married sixty years today. Been together for sixty-two." I melted.

"May I be nosy and ask how you met?" Whenever I meet old couples, there's usually a story or two to tell. Why should this couple be any different? The woman laughed and that's when I noticed she was missing a few teeth on the sides of her mouth. She still had her front teeth and she seemed to be doing just fine on her fish filet and fries, bless her heart.

"She was a damned criminal!" he exclaimed. They both laughed and she lightly slapped his shoulder. "No, really. She was." His eyes went to hers and there was nothing but pure love between them. Hallmark, eat your heart out.

"Okay, I'll bite. What kind of nefarious deeds was she guilty of sixty-two years ago?" I was more than willing to play along with this adorable couple. I worked on my meal as he started his story.

"I was a new trooper back in the day. I was full of piss and vinegar and wanted to impress my superiors, so I was out there writing tickets all day and night. I gave some people a break now and then, but when you're trying to make a name for yourself, you just write until your hand cramps." He shook his right hand and flexed his fingers a few times. "One day I was just north of Burlington, and I saw this Chevy chugging along. It wasn't going too fast, so I couldn't write the driver for speeding. Then I noticed the car was weaving. A little to the right, a little to the left. Now mind you, we didn't have the big highways back then like we do now. Still, that weaving in and out was reason enough to pull that dangerous car over and see what was going on." He had a hard time keeping his face straight.

The whole time he was telling his story, she was just sitting back, nibbling on her fries, and looking at him with hearts in her eyes. I was pretty sure this was not the first time they'd told their story.

"For the record, I was NOT weaving in and out and driving like a maniac. I may have gone over the middle line once or twice. But I was by no means swerving like a blind, drunken fool."

She pointed a french fry at him as she was stating that last sentence. He tried to bite it out of her fingers but missed.

"So, I lit her up. I pulled her over, stepped out of my car, and put my hat on. I was taller back then and couldn't wear my hat in the car. Not enough room. Anyway, I walked up to the driver's side of the car waiting to tussle with some drunk. But that's not what I saw. Before I could even ask for her license and registration, I was in shock." He looked at his bride of sixty years and they shared a knowing giggle.

"Well? C'mon. Was she falling asleep? Playing with the radio? What?" I asked.

In fits and spurts he finally told me, "She had a beagle in the front seat with her. A momma beagle. Well, she was becoming a momma right at that moment. All over the front seat, all over her lap." He started laughing as he swooshed his hands around her lap area.

"I was young. I thought my dog needed help delivering because she was whining, standing, then stretching out on the floor, then getting back up. I thought my dad could help, so I loaded her into the car and headed out to see my folks. I didn't know she was going to give birth in my front seat and on me!" She was wailing and laughing at the same time.

"I looked inside the window and the first thing I saw was blood on her lap, so I thought she was hurt. Then I quickly saw three or four tiny squirming bodies on her lap and a couple sitting next to her. The look on her pretty little face was priceless." He patted her lap as if to show me exactly where the dog had delivered her precious cargo.

I started laughing. "So what was her terrible crime? Kidnapping? Dognapping?"

The man looked me dead in the eye and said, "She stole my heart. I had to give her a life sentence." At that moment they both laughed then kissed a quick peck.

They went on to tell me how the dog ended up delivering seven puppies in total. The kindly trooper had a blanket in his trunk, so he proceeded to move momma dog and her pups into the back seat. He then escorted this messy-lapped lady to where her parents lived and helped her put the dogs in the barn. She invited him in to meet her mom and dad. They approved immediately.

"He insisted on getting my name and address to make sure I wasn't too rattled after this huge puppy ordeal." She winked at me.

"What can I say? It was a gory sight. You could have been traumatized. I was only doing my duty by following up and checking on you." Straight face, but his eyes gave him away.

They ended up keeping two of the puppies. They named one Trooper and the other one Lap. They found good homes for the rest of the beagle pups.

The rain had finally let up. I was finished with my meal and still had three hours to go before I could pull into my driveway, so I said my good-byes. They smiled and wished me a safe trip home. As I headed toward the door, I was grinning. I made a detour to the counter and bought a gift card. I walked back over to the couple and handed them the card and wished them another happy sixty years together. At that comment they thanked me, smiled, and said they'd do their doggone best!

THE FLUTE

"War is Hell," Cary stated. "That may be a cliché, but it's true. You'll notice most guys who have seen real action won't ever talk about it." Cary squinted his light blue eyes as he looked off into the uncut hay field. We sat on the rickety old back porch that was attached to his ramshackle farmhouse. The funny thing is, I never felt unsafe at Cary's house even though it looked like it was going to fall in on itself at any moment. I think that had to do with Cary. He exuded strength and resilience and it seemed to ease into his surroundings and seep into the people next to him. I can't say I've ever felt so safe and protected as I did when I was in Cary's orbit.

I watched as Cary flipped the cap off another Budweiser bottle and took a long pull from it. He was right. Most guys who have seen the horrors of war won't talk about it. Today was different. As the sun made its way across the sky and inched toward sunset, it was clear my friend wanted to talk. He wiped the condensation from the bottle onto his worn jeans.

"Not like I had a choice, mind you. I was drafted. I had a good job, but I was just twenty years old, and ripe for the pickin'." He scratched the side of his weathered face with his hand. I noticed a slight tremor. Was that from years of alcohol or drugs? Not my business. "I was so green. I mean really green. I hunted deer and turkeys when I was a kid, but never in my life did I think I'd ever have to hunt a human. It does something to a man." His whisker-stubbled jaw clenched for a few seconds. I knew he didn't expect me to hold up my end of the conversation. This was all him. This was his moment to get some feelings that had been tamped way down into his soul out into the sunlight, no matter how painful that would be. So I sat. I looked at him, or off into the field when his eyes would fill with tears. The man still had pride. I wasn't going to take that away from him. "They tore us all away from our homes, our towns, our families. We didn't know what we were facing. Oh sure, we'd heard stories, but nothing prepares you for war. Not really. It's not like the movies. It's a lot worse." Another swig from the bottle. "I can't tell you about the bad stuff. I still can't talk about the really horrible things we did or saw. Those nightmares will die with me." Cary shook his head slightly and I thought I saw him shiver.

"But let me tell you about one good thing that happened. Yeah, I know that sounds stupid, but out of all that mess over there in Vietnam, there was something good that happened."

I stood up a little bit and moved my chair around so I was facing him. I wanted to give Cary my full attention. Obviously, this was a tiny ray of light in a very dark place in his life, and I wanted him to know I valued his trust in me. I sat and waited.

"First off, you know I was named after that movie star Cary Grant, right? My mother was totally in love with Cary Grant. She thought he was the most handsome and dapper man in the world. My father would laugh it off and tell her if she ever ran away with Cary Grant, he'd understand." He giggled at the thought of that ever happening. "And I gotta tell you, as I grew up, I may have combed my hair like Cary Grant did. I might have picked up a few of his mannerisms. He was just THAT guy, you know?" I knew. Even though Cary Grant was more popular in my mother's era, I still appreciated that fine man. "But I didn't end up as nice as that Cary. I only wish I had."

"It was hot. It was hot and swampy. We were clearing a small village one evening, and most of the people had run away into the high grass or woods. Hell, you can call it a jungle. By the time we'd gotten to this village, we were all tired and wrung out. We didn't want to be there; we knew those people had nothing to do with the war. But we had our orders to clear the village. We made lots of noise before we got there. It was almost as if

15

we wanted to give them a head start so we wouldn't have to do the unthinkable. Again. Of course, I'm telling you it was 'almost' like that because anything more than that would be disobeying direct orders from the head honchos calling the shots. So take from it what you will . . ." Cary's voice trailed off.

He pushed up his shirt sleeves revealing faded military tattoos on both forearms. Reaching into the cooler, he pulled out another Bud and opened it. "The village was so small. It was more like a settlement, or a camp. These people had nothing. Barely the basics. They ran, they screamed. We emptied their little shacks. I tell you, a man can feel pretty small as he's tearing apart another man's home, even if it's built out of just a few sticks." He shook his head slightly as the memories came flooding back. "I crouched down and walked into one of the huts and started tossing things outside. A thin blanket, a small table, a couple of mats on the floor. I reached for a bundle of clothes and that's when I saw her eyes." Cary shifted in his chair then cleared his throat. "I had one hand on my rifle, and the other hand gripping this little girl's shirt. She couldn't have been more than six or seven years old. The terror in her big brown eyes screamed at me even though she was silent. And I knew, at that moment, what I had to do."

My heart sank. My eyes started filling with tears. What this man was expected to do was beyond anything anyone should ever be asked to do. I sat frozen in my chair.

"I looked down at this little girl, and she had something in her hand. It was a piece of wood. She slowly raised it up, holding it in front of her. Then she stretched her little arm out and offered it to me. It was a flute. Well, I guess that's as close as you could get to describing it. Probably the only toy the kid had. She was handing it to me, almost as if in trade for her life. This child knew I had the power and strength to end her short years here on Earth, and she was trying to make a deal with the Devil. That's what it felt like."

I was silently bawling. I couldn't even see. The tears were rushing down my cheeks, off my jaw, and onto my shirt.

"This child was offering me the only possession she had on Earth. So I took it. I eased my grip on her shirt and slowly lowered her to the ground. I threw a couple of tattered blankets over her and pressed my index finger to my lips and gave her a shhh. She nodded. We didn't speak the same language, but she understood."

My breath was shallow, and I was still crying but not saying a word.

"I put her little flute in my pocket and walked out of that hut. My sergeant looked at me and asked if it was clear. I said yes, and we moved on. I'll never know what happened to that kid or her family, but I hope they made it."

"You did the right thing, Cary. No doubt about it. Whether she made it for one more day or if she's still alive today, you did what was right." I reached over and put a hand on his shoulder and gave it a squeeze. This story didn't go where I thought it was going, and for that, I was grateful.

"Hold on a second. I gotta go take a leak. Be right back." He stepped inside and was gone for a few minutes. I stared out into the field and had even more appreciation for the silence and peace within my view.

Cary came back out to the porch and sat down. "My grandson plays all those friggin' video games. He thinks it's cool to shoot people and blow up buildings. He tells me when he's old enough, he's going to join the Marines so he can wipe out the bad guys. He's not old enough to know what's what. One of these days when he's older, I'm going to have a sit-down with him. It's one thing to be patriotic. It's another thing to be stupid. Even though we weren't treated that good back then, I wouldn't have done it differently. I'm an American. I do what my country asks of me and I do it with pride. War is never the answer, but sometimes it's the only way. You have to get that through your head, otherwise it'll eat you up alive."

I nodded. "I regret not serving my country, Cary. I graduated from high school, had a couple of crappy jobs, and then I got into a great job. I'll be there until I retire. I know I'm one of the lucky ones but, still, I wish I'd signed up to serve at least four years."

"Well, the universe had other plans for you, honey. You would have done fine in the service. But in a way, I'm glad you didn't go. You never know what you're going to have to face. That's part of the deal when you sign up. You have to go into it knowing it's not all roses. You just have to do your duty, do what they ask of you, and remember you're a good citizen, a good American."

We sat there for another fifteen minutes or so, just watching the reddish sun set on the horizon. I looked over at Cary and was about to say good-bye to him when I noticed he had something in his hands. He was holding a small wooden object. It was about eight inches long and had holes in it. It was the flute. Cary looked at me and held the flute up in front of his face and said, "One of these days I'll explain this to my grandson. Hopefully he'll understand. I'd appreciate it if you didn't say anything. At least not until I'm dead."

I stood up and so did Cary. I hugged him and wiped my tears on his shoulder.

EASY BREAD

What would my book be without at least one easy recipe to try? Below is a recipe I stumbled upon a few years back. There's nothing fancy about it. It's just plain ol' white bread. What I like about it is its simplicity. It's quick to throw together and it's easy to add in different ingredients to change it up a bit. Sometimes I toss in a teaspoon or two of crushed herbs like rosemary or thyme. If I'm making rolls, I might stir in some crushed garlic or maybe some Parmesan cheese. Whether you make loaves of bread or rolls, they'll turn out perfectly every time and with very little effort. Enjoy!

White Bread

Mix together:
1 cup of all-purpose flour
3 Tablespoons of sugar
2 1/4 teaspoons of yeast
1 cup of warm water

Let this rest at least 10 minutes to activate the yeast. Then add:
3 Tablespoons of olive or vegetable oil
1 cup of flour
1 1/2 teaspoons of salt

Mix well. NOTE: If adding herbs, garlic, or other goodies, stir them in now.

Add:
1 cup of flour

Mix, knead, and let rise in one loaf pan or two mini loaf pans for 30 minutes. (You can also form into rolls of any size, just be attentive to baking time.)

Bake at 375°F for 25-30 minutes for the loaf of bread (less time for the mini loaves and rolls; just bake until the tops are light brown).

THE CASHEW TEST

A two-hour layover in Chicago's O'Hare turned into a four-hour delay. I guess lightning storms have more authority than the control tower when it comes to letting people get into metal tubes that zing through the sky at super high speeds. I didn't need to get to Las Vegas that night. The wedding I was attending wasn't until two days later, so there was plenty of time. Still, four hours sitting in an airport can make one's chest heave a heavy sigh.

It was a little after 7:00 p.m. and I hadn't eaten anything for dinner yet. I was counting on the light snack the airline was going to provide but that plan was out the window now. Instead, I meandered down past the gift shops and newsstands until I came to a small restaurant. It wasn't a fast-food joint, so it was relatively quiet. Just the way I like it. I walked in and the hostess said they weren't seating anyone in the dining room, but they were serving the bar menu if I cared to sit up there. She nodded her auburn-topped head toward the horseshoe-shaped bar that currently held only four patrons. I told her, "Thank you, that's perfect." I walked over to the end stool furthest away from the television. I don't like a lot of noise when I'm eating. I don't need to hear about the latest murder or train wreck while I'm trying to ingest and digest. The gentleman tending bar came over and placed a small square light green napkin in front of me and asked me what I'd care to drink. Since I had four hours to kill, I asked for a Coors Light. Nothing too heavy. Besides, it's not like I was driving, right? He came back with a frosty mug of Coors Light and a bar menu. Two of the other patrons were just leaving and two remained, what I presumed was a husband-wife couple. I perused the menu and ordered a bacon burger.

The bartender was probably in his upper 60's but held it quite well. He reminded me of a shorter Sam Elliott in the respect that he was obviously very handsome as a young man and grew even more so as he aged. Some guys just look better and better with the onset of those gray hairs and deep facial lines. His voice was deep, but not quite as deep as Mr. Elliott's. I tried to hide my disappointment about his voice as he placed my burger in front of me and asked if he could get me anything else. I smiled and said, "No, everything looks perfect."

Just then, the couple that was left at the bar started having a loud discussion. It was plain to see they were at each other's throats and none too happy. She'd hiss at him through clenched teeth, and he bobbed his head toward her to accentuate every syllable of his rant. This went on for a couple of minutes, then they realized they were in a very public place. The man reached for his wallet, pulled some cash out, and laid it on the bar. He then reached down and picked up his carry-on bag and started walking out of the bar. His woman reluctantly followed, glancing back at the bartender for only a second with an embarrassed "I'm sorry" look on her face.

"Wow. That was a bit of a touchy moment, huh?" I said to my shorter Sam.

"Oh yes. We get a few in here now and then. It's stressful to travel. I see worse than that, believe me." He shook his head and proceeded to clear the couple's plates and wipe the bar clean. He then came back to me and in a non-flirty way, asked me if I had a husband. I told him no, the right one hadn't crossed my path yet. He chuckled.

"May I give you a little advice? You know, so you don't end up like that?" He nodded his head where that arguing couple had just been seated. "It's free advice. But remember, you get what you pay for." He gave me a quick wink and a smirk.

"Hit me with it. Let me hear your sage advice for this weary traveler!" I chomped down on my bacon burger and chewed silently as he squared up and imparted his bit of wisdom.

"I've been a marriage counselor for over thirty-five years," he began.

"Wait. You're a marriage counselor? What are you doing here bartending in a busy airport?" I was confused.

"Marriage counselor, bartender, they're interchangeable. Same thing–only my tips as a bartender are much better than if I had a framed piece of paper on the wall saying I'm qualified by a school to listen to your problems." He gave me a brilliant smile.

Ahh, I get it. So he has a bit of humor too. Love it. He continued on with a few things he saw as a bartender. "I could write a book on what to look out for if you're a guy and I could write another book for the women. It never ceases to amaze me what people will tell bartenders. Or even worse, what people will say to each other, right in front of me! It's almost like they don't realize I can see them and that I have ears." He shook his head and rolled his eyes. "I'm not hurrying you out of here, but I only have another twenty minutes on the clock, so I'll make this lesson brief. When you're interested in someone, do the cashew test. I do this for fun when couples come in and sit down."

I was still working on my big bacon burger and gave a small grunt and a shrug of my shoulder as if to say please go on. I couldn't talk with my mouth full, but I really wanted to hear about his cashew test.

"We serve salty treats for free at the bar so people will buy more drinks. It's standard practice. Sometimes popcorn, sometimes pretzels. On a slow night I'll put out the mixed nuts because they're a little more costly, but still salty. If I see a couple come in and I'm in a playful mood, I'll ask if they have a nut allergy, or is it okay to serve a bowl of mixed nuts. Nobody has had an allergy yet, so I'll set a bowl of mixed nuts down between them. Then I watch. If the guy reaches in first without pushing the bowl toward the woman offering her first dibs, that's a red flag. Same with the woman. I like seeing them both reach for the bowl and dip in at the same time. Once in a while it happens but

23

not always. Now, if you'll notice, mixed nut combinations are usually a lot of peanuts because they're cheaper. Then you've got your better nuts in there–a few walnuts, maybe some pecans, or almonds. Then you'll find a small percentage of those delectable cashews. Those are gold, right? I sit back and watch to see who reaches in and snags all the cashews out before the other person can get them. Not to pick on my fellow brothers, but men seem to feel more entitled, and that air of superiority hangs around them like tinsel on a Christmas tree! If I see a guy reach into the bowl and pick out all the best nuts, all the cashews, I guarantee he's one selfish bastard at home. I'd bet my bottom dollar he has the better vehicle, the better clothes, man toys, and so on."

I nodded and thought about this. He could see my mind churning as I looked back on a few of my relationships and although there weren't any bowls of mixed nuts, there were other kinds of "cashews" that were picked out of the mix.

"If the woman reaches in first and scarfs all the cashews, she's a guaranteed high maintenance woman who will never be satisfied with whatever she gets. It'll never be enough." I thought this was a pretty broad statement. Maybe not everyone likes cashews. Maybe it didn't matter to some people if their mate took the best that was offered and left them peanuts. Still, it was an interesting theory. Then my own words sank into my head: Their mate took the best that was offered and left them with peanuts. This sentence played in my mind several times.

I finished my meal, paid the tab, and tipped Almost Sam generously. I thanked him for the conversation and advice. I picked up my backpack and headed toward gate C-14. I decided to be more observant for a few weeks. Whenever I was around couples I knew, I'd watch to see who picked the better steak off the grill, who sat in the more comfortable chair, who took the bench in the shade on a hot day. And damn it, wasn't he right? He could see this with total strangers and with only minutes to observe. He was scarily accurate, and I was impressed.

Fortunately, I know a few couples who don't take the cashews. Several couples I know have such a strong respect for each other that it's more of a fight to see which one could give the other the cashews (figuratively speaking now, of course). I love seeing couples who genuinely care to see their partners happy. The love and admiration that's given back and forth in those couples makes me believe in forever. I know those couples will go the distance. I still do a bit of people-watching, especially couples. I'm always going to be a busybody when it comes to observing people around me. Now, if you'll excuse me, I have to run to the store to get another can of mixed nuts for my company coming over tomorrow night.

DID HE, OR DIDN'T HE?

I had three brothers, but only the eldest is alive at this time. Tyler was the third child out of six, and definitely marched to a different drummer than the first two kids. Tyler was a rebel. He didn't like school, picked up the cigarette habit as a teen, and quickly learned how wonderful adult beverages could be. Of course, he also enjoyed that special herb so many teenagers were fond of in those days. It's still quite popular and was recently made legal. Oh, how Tyler must be laughing now. Although we had rules in our home, Tyler didn't care to notice or obey them. I think my parents just got tired of fighting him and let him do whatever he wanted. The teen years are hell on any parent.

One day Tyler decided he wanted to buy a motorcycle. He was still in high school and dearly wanted a bike. He had saved his money then eventually bought a big old Allstate motorcycle. It wasn't new and it didn't have a lot of bells and whistles on it, but it was a motorcycle and it ran. Tyler loved that machine and rode it around the back fields and up and down our back road as much as he could. He didn't have the money to get it registered or insured, so the folks told him to stay off the road and to be careful. You can guess where I'm going with this, can't you?

One evening, Tyler decided to ride his motorcycle down to the Brasher Iron Works. Actually, it was the Smith District of the Iron Works where his girlfriend lived. He scooted down there, only about five miles from the farm, to see his sweetie. On his way back he was pulled over by a trooper. Oops. No helmet.

No insurance. No registration. No motorcycle license. That poor trooper had cramps in his hand by the time he finished writing all the tickets Tyler had earned that night. The trooper wouldn't even let him ride his bike the one mile to get home. Tyler had to knock on a neighbor's door and call our folks. After he explained what happened, my father drove his pickup truck down the road, loaded up the motorcycle, and drove back to the farm in silence.

The folks were livid. They had warned Tyler to stay off the roads, especially the main road where there was much more traffic. But hey, the heart wants what the heart wants, right? And his heart was down in the Smith District of the Iron Works. A few weeks went by and my father took Tyler to the town court. He was given a lecture by the Justice of the Peace and a bit of a fine for each ticket written. Tyler was ashamed, embarrassed, and angry. In his mind, it was just a bike. Just a few miles. Nobody got hurt. He rationalized it in so many ways in his head. It wasn't HIS fault, right? My father paid the fines and they went home.

This didn't sit well with Tyler. He stewed about it. He thought he was being picked on by "THE MAN" and wanted to strike back. His mind churned with ideas on how he could retaliate against what he thought was an unfair punishment for him which, money-wise, was passed on to our father. And then it hit him. Much like how the Grinch came up with the plan to steal Christmas from the Whos in Whoville, Tyler had a plan to get back at the strict town Justice.

Now, I hadn't heard this story until many years after Tyler's death in 1985, so I have no way of confirming or denying if it really happened. My younger brother Tim told me this story about ten years ago, but Tim's dead now so it's up to me whether I believe it. I'm 99.9% sure this DID happen, but maybe that tiny percentage of me wants to think it was just wishful thinking on Tyler's part.

The story goes like this: One late night Tyler went out to the back field where he was growing his own herbs, and he dug one up and placed it in a bag. He then hopped on his still illegal motorcycle and drove it in the direction of the Justice's home. He parked his bike off the road and walked to the backyard of the Justice's house. Tyler then planted his special herb in the JP's flower garden. He then stealthily trotted back to his hidden motorcycle and headed home.

Nothing was ever mentioned about this little midnight jaunt of his. If my parents had known about this, his head would have been on a platter. Tyler kept his secret for a few years, then eventually told Tim. It was many years later that Tim told me about Tyler's little escapade in the Justice of the Peace's flower garden. I laughed. It sure sounds like something my brother would have done. Did he really do it? I'm going with that 99.9%.

PULL THE SHADES

Bitter grief sits heavily in the center of my heart
Knowing your voice is silent now.
Never again will I feel the soft caress of your fingertips upon my face.
Your loving arms embracing me will not be forgotten.
The lifetime of laughter and tears we shared
Now feels like only a brief moment.
How did the years escape us so quickly?
Why didn't anyone show us how to slow time?
My memories desperately reach out
To hold you for one more precious minute,
But I'm denied that comfort.
Losing you means losing the best part of myself.
My body and soul will never be whole again.
There is no longer light in my life without you next to me.
I pull the shades on the windows of my heart
For, without you, my very essence is shrouded in darkness.

MA'S CIRCUS
PEANUTS

I suppose one drawback to dying is that you can't stand up for yourself or deny any accusations the ones you leave behind say about you. Then again, in the case of my mother, she can't take any credit for her shenanigans either. You already know about the grocery store trips and how I still get flashbacks whenever I see those pepperoni sticks and 40-lb. bags of flour. I'd like to add another story to the list of things that make me remember my mother and her warped sense of humor.

My mother's favorite candy was that marshmallow confection known as circus peanuts. Soft, orange, and shaped like a big peanut, they could be found in any store at any time. Those circus peanuts weren't a holiday special like candy canes or jellybeans; you could get this chewy delight any ol' time you wanted. Once all of us kids were grown up and moved out of the house, finances were a little better for the folks. Still, it wasn't often my mother would splurge on herself and get a bag of circus peanuts. On the rare occasion she did, she'd start nibbling on a few, then keep reaching back into the bag for "just one more" which always turned into several more. She'd offer them to anyone sitting at the table and more often than not, the others would politely decline. Sometimes I could even see the suppression of a gag reflex. I believe circus peanuts are like Halloween's candy corn. You either love 'em or hate 'em. No in-between.

One day I was in the grocery store in Massena and was

30

going to visit my folks when I finished picking up a few things I needed. As I was headed toward the checkout, I spotted a bag of circus peanuts and thought, "Hey, Ma would like a nice little treat." I tossed the bag into my cart and checked out. When I arrived at the farm and walked into the kitchen with that bag of candy in my hand, my mother's eyes lit up. "OH! You brought me some puke peanuts!" I cocked my head to one side and an eyebrow twitched upward.

"PUKE peanuts?" I asked.

"Yes, I call them puke peanuts because they're just so good that I could eat them until I puked then eat some more!" She grinned.

"Oh, I get it. Well, good thing you never push it that far, huh?"

"I haven't yet. But there's always a first time!" Then she laughed.

I sat down and we had a great chat about everything that had been going on in my life, at my job, and how my home improvements had been coming along–new paint here, new carpet there, and so on. Ma opened the bag of circus, I mean PUKE peanuts, and inhaled that sickeningly sweet aroma. "Ahhh! This is what heaven must smell like," she sighed. I ate a couple but that's about my limit. Obviously, I hadn't worked up a good constitution to puke peanuts. Such an amateur.

Fast forward a couple of years later. My mother had some health issues and one of those was a frail immune system. Whenever she caught even a slight cold, it turned into pneumonia. She'd cough and wheeze so hard I'd swear a lung was going to come flying out of her mouth at any given moment. Watching her gasp for breath while turning purple was horrifying. She always waited until it was too late and ended up in the emergency room, admitted to the hospital for three to six days. Her poor doctor would come in and look at her, tsk-tsk-ing and shaking his head. In his Indian accent he'd say, "Now Marilyn (he said it like 'Med-i-lin'), you know you cannot wait this long when you have a cold. You know you cannot fix it yourself. We have been through this (he pronounced as 'true dis') many a time before. Do not wait. Please help me help you." My mother would nod her oxygen-masked face and promise she wouldn't wait too long again.

She lied.

This one time she caught a cold and was actually feeling a little better at first. She remembered promising her doctor she wouldn't wait too long, but this time felt different. She KNEW she could kick it on her own. For the first couple of days, it wasn't bad–mild headache, a bit of a cough, some congestion. By the third day she was coughing a little more and had lost her appetite. The only things that tasted good to her were coffee and her beloved circus peanuts. By the fourth day she was sounding like a 1957 Electrolux vacuum cleaner that had been left on in a gravel pit. I could hear the air going in and mixing it up in her lungs like she was crushing pebbles in a blender. Not good. She was super weak and couldn't even get off the couch to get to the car, so my father called the rescue squad immediately. He figured they'd know how to get air into her if she stopped breathing, which was a very good (and scary) possibility at that moment.

The ambulance arrived and three young men jumped out; they grabbed their gear bags and the stretcher. They came into the house, assessed the situation, and put my mother on her to-go cart. They had an oxygen mask on her and as they were wheeling her out of the house, she pulled the mask aside for a second and said, "I need to sit up." They told her no, she had to stay lying down, and they placed the mask back over her face. Again, she reached up and tried to roll to one side to prop her head and shoulders up a little bit. "I (gasp!) need to (wheeze!) sit up!" Again, they said no, and they pushed her head and shoulders flat on the stretcher. They'd made it to the ambulance in the driveway and just as they lifted her inside, she reached up one more time, pulled the oxygen mask off, and proceeded to throw up all over the ambulance's bench seats, floor, stretcher, and the pants of one of the volunteers. That was bad enough but, to make matters worse, the ONLY thing she had eaten all day was . . . yup . . . puke peanuts and coffee. So there in the back of the Tri-Town Rescue Squad was a Ghostbusters-like fluorescent orange SLIME splattered all over the place. She looked at the rescue squad guys and tried to apologize, but all she got out was, "I TOLD YOU I HAD TO SIT UP!" If she'd been sitting up, gravity wouldn't have allowed that orange puddle of semi-digested puke peanuts to come up her throat and exit her wheezing orifice.

Those guys were champs. They didn't bat an eye. They propped the head of the stretcher up a little bit, just enough to deter any further orange spew from escaping my mother. In all honesty, she resembled Linda Blair in *The Exorcist*–different color, but same impressive results. Ma was carted off to the emergency room in Massena, and the whole "you waited too long" speech from her doctor was given.

After a few days she was released with a prescription for antibiotics and was told to rest, drink plenty of fluids, and to eat regular food, not just candy. Of course, there was no mercy for her once we knew she was going to be fine. We busted on her about being serious when she called them PUKE peanuts. We told her we believed her and she didn't have to prove her point, but she did anyway. She took it all in good stride and with a grin. She continued to eat puke peanuts until her last days here. When she died, I snagged a little bag of puke peanuts from Stewart's and tucked them into her casket. I thought she might appreciate a little snack for the ride.

Ma has been gone for 20 years. And just like the pepperoni and big bags of flour, whenever I see a bag of puke peanuts, I laugh and send up a "hi" to her. Once in a while I'll get a small bag and take them to the cemetery where she's buried. I'll sit down, chat with her, eat a few puke peanuts, then place the rest on her grave.

GUT FEELING

How many times have you had that "gut feeling" about a person, place, or situation? Sometimes it's just so strong you can't ignore it. I'll bet if you thought about it for a bit, you could come up with several times in your life that you're glad you listened to your gut. Your inner self was warning you about something or someone. On the contrary, have there been times when you were given a message but decided to ignore it? What happened then? Oh yeah. You ended up terribly disappointed or hurt. Maybe you lost money, or you were used in some way. Invariably, you utter those fateful words, "I shoulda listened to my gut!"

Ever since I was a young girl, I "knew" on some level that I didn't want to bear children. It wasn't that I hated kids or couldn't stand being around them. There was just something deep down inside me that said getting pregnant and having a child was not on my To-Do list. When I was in my early 20's, I had my tubes cut and cauterized. The doctor who did it went out of his way to make me feel like a total whore. His exact words were, "You just want to have all the fun and no responsibility!" I tried to explain to him that there are already plenty of children born who need homes. I gave statistics about the foster care system and how many children were abandoned by their biological parents. I explained IF and when I ever wanted a child, I'd get one that was already born who needed a good home with plenty of love. I also listed the hereditary diseases that abound in my family tree. Cancer, epilepsy, Alzheimer's, heart conditions, scleroderma, and so on. He thought those were flimsy excuses.

Then I realized he was the only OB/GYN guy in town and young, fertile women like me were his bread and butter. How DARE I take money out of his pocket by not reproducing? In the end, he did the laparoscopic tubal ligation. My insurance didn't cover it, so I paid out of pocket. (Note: they paid for vasectomies, but not tubal ligations.)

I've never regretted my decision to not have children. I've thoroughly enjoyed spoiling other peoples' kids including the ones in my own family. Sometimes it's fun to be the crazy aunt who can take you on a wild vacation. I have numerous friends and former co-workers who have children and I've spoiled them whenever I've had the chance. I've supported more children's school fundraisers than if I'd had my own little ones. There's no way I could ever add up how many boxes of greeting cards, buckets of cookie dough, packages of kitchen utensils, and magazine subscriptions I've purchased through my friends' kids. I've never said no to any raffle tickets for whatever sport the child was playing. I've opened my heart and checkbook for every graduation, from kindergarten to college. The bridal showers, weddings, and baby showers followed all the school fundraisers. I happily supported each child and felt I was doing my share. If it takes a village, I was definitely in that neighborhood.

Over the years I've been mocked, scolded, and put down for my decision to not reproduce. I never understood how my womb affected other people. I was told I was selfish. I was asked, "Who's going to take care of you when you get old?" Wow. I wouldn't wish that on anyone, especially a loved one. I tried to ignore those cutting remarks and put-downs. All I knew was, deep down, somewhere in my soul, I didn't need to have babies.

Fast forward to December of 1997. The guy I was dating at the time was driving us into town to go see the latest Sigourney Weaver *Alien* movie. We were almost to the theater and I started having wicked pains in my stomach. (How appropriate, considering the movie we were going to see.) The pain started radiating out toward my ribcage and to my back. Even my shoulders started aching. My heart was pounding. I had never felt that kind of pain before in my life. I looked at my boyfriend and through the tears told him to drive me to the emergency room . . . NOW! One look at my sweaty face and shaking body and knew I was in trouble. He floored it. We arrived at the hospital, and he carried me in and laid me on a stretcher. I could barely talk; the pain was so bad. They asked a few questions (name, age, could I be pregnant?) and then realized I was going into shock from the pain. One nurse in particular was really fantastic. She kept calm and cool and when the doctor told her to give me some Demerol, she softly but firmly looked me in the eye and said, "I'm going to give you something for the pain, but we need to put an IV in your arm." I nodded and held still as best I could. Within a minute that glorious Demerol was coursing through my veins and the excruciating pain magically disappeared. I could breathe again.

Once I was calmed down and under control, the doctor ordered an ultrasound. The nurse wheeled me into another room and the technician came in and sat beside me. She asked a few questions then got right to it. She squeezed some gooey lube on my stomach and moved the wand around. She clicked the keyboard and froze the monitor a few times, making notes. I couldn't really see what she was doing, but that was fine with me. That sweet drug was really smoothing me out. You could have pierced my nipples with a rusty nail at that point and I would have said that's fine. (Thankfully, nobody did.) After a few swipes up and down my stomach area, the technician asked me to roll over on my side. She then eased the wand up and down on my back. "Roll over to your other side, please." I did. Same thing. Up and down that side of my back.

Finally, she rested the wand on the upper part of my abdomen. That's when she told me I definitely had a problem with my gallbladder. Apparently a stone had lodged in the opening that takes the bile out of the gallbladder and I was "backing up" in fluid which caused me considerable pain. (I really like that expression. Considerable pain. HA!)

Then she lowered the wand to just below my belly button.

She clicked the keyboard of her computer and took a few pictures.

"Did you realize you have an abdominal kidney?" The technician waited for me to answer. I looked at her like she had three heads.

She asked again. "Did you know you have a kidney in the front?"

"Uhhh, no. How is that possible? Is it an extra? Is it working? Do I have to have it removed? Is it causing some of this pain?" I had at least a dozen more questions, all flying out of my drug-induced happiness.

"No, it's not an extra one. That's why I was checking your back. You have one kidney in the back, and this one here in the front. It's working fine. No need to remove it. However, if you ever donate a kidney, this is the one to take. It would be much easier to harvest than the one in the back."

This was not computing. In my mind I was thinking *so what you're telling me is if someone were to punch me in the gut, that would be a kidney shot?* The Rocky fan in me had questions. The chances of me being punched in the gut, or anywhere for that matter, were pretty much nil. But Demerol doesn't care about that.

The bearer of weird news then wiped the goo off my belly and back and returned me to the emergency room. She shared her findings with the nurses and doctor on duty. They huddled around saying things like, "No shit! I've never seen THAT before!" or "Hey, this is only the second time I've seen this in my 20-year career!" Cool. I'm a freak.

I was scheduled for surgery the next morning. The handsome young surgeon came in and gave me the scoop. He'd be taking my gallbladder out and I'd feel MUCH better. Four little cuts in my belly area and I'd be good to go. Thank you!

Then he looked at me and asked, "You've never had children, have you?"

I looked at him oddly. I hadn't disclosed my prior surgery to him. I've found it's sometimes better NOT to bring that topic up to some people. Obviously they did a pregnancy test on me when I arrived and again to make sure I wasn't going under his knife with a little one growing inside me. That's something the docs really want to know before they put you under and start carving.

"No, I don't have any kids. I prefer to spoil other peoples' kids," I said with a grin.

"Well, it's your decision, but it's probably a good thing you don't have children. With your abdominal kidney, that could be a problem. If you were to carry a child, your uterus would push against that kidney and possibly rupture it. You could also have issues with arteries and blood vessels if you were to get pregnant. There are several things that could go very wrong for you. Again, it's your decision, but if you want to have children, this is something to consider."

I thanked him for his opinion and let him know I was good to go on the gallbladder removal.

When all was said and done, I DID feel like a million bucks! No more horrible pains in my belly area. I felt like a new woman. Even my boyfriend at the time admitted he was very worried. He said, "Pendra, I knew you were in horrible pain. When they said they'd give you some medicine to stop the pain, but they'd have to give it to you in an IV, you threw your arm out and yelled 'HURRY!' to the nurse. That's when I knew you were definitely in trouble. I know how much you hate needles, but when you ASKED for an IV, that was the clincher!" He was right. I'm a total wuss when it comes to needles. I do remember thrusting my arm out to that nurse. That lovely angel.

Every now and then I wonder if my body knew I shouldn't ever get pregnant and somehow warned me. How did I instinctively know I should get snipped in my 20's? I was 36 years old when my gallbladder acted up and I had my first ultrasound. That was the moment I found out about my abdominal kidney. Thirty-six years of total ignorance of my own internal organs. And yet, somehow my body told me to be careful. It told me what not to do. I listened to my gut feeling.

GRIEF

Grief. It's a tough one. We all face it. Nobody escapes it. Ever.

Wise people will tell you about balance in life. They'll say you can't have pleasure without pain. Can't have the heat without the cold. Everything has an opposite and in order to appreciate all the good things in life, we must experience a few of the bad things too. Kinda sucks, doesn't it? I'd like to think I could appreciate having all good things happen to me. Then again, maybe that's because I've tasted what I think is my fair share of that bitter brew called grief.

When we're young we're so much more resilient. I remember my heart being torn up when I'd see a dead barn cat. After a few days my short attention span would move on to other, more important events. The sharp pain of seeing the deceased cat would ease up, soften, then disintegrate somewhere in my heart and mind. This was a recurring play as a child growing up on a farm. Animals came, animals went. We buried the pets and my father "took care of" the barn cats or other critters who may have decided to stop breathing in our paths. More than once I remember Oscar taking an old grain sack and sliding a cat, raccoon, or squirrel into it and setting it aside to be taken to the back field later that evening. Such is the circle of life. Even coyotes have to eat.

I think there are different kinds of grief. There's the relief grief. That's when someone you love is sick or injured and there's no way they're ever going to get better. Could be your mom, dad, child, spouse, friend, or longtime pet. Yes, I'm including animals in this because I'm positive pets give the most unconditional love there is. So there you are, watching this important piece of your heart suffer in pain. It could take minutes; it could take years. We've all witnessed both. I'm betting I'm not the only person who has tried to breathe for someone who was struggling for air. I can't tell you the number of times I would inhale deeply as my mother would take shallow gasps, the oxygen tubes up her nose not helping very much. Feeling helpless while watching someone you love die is torture. You know they don't want you to suffer too, but that's how grief works. Eventually, the last breath is taken and life slips away from its mortal package. Tears are wept, noses blown, hands held. And yet, somewhere deep down inside us, we're relieved. We're glad we don't have to witness the pain and torment anymore. We're relieved the suffering is over for the person or pet who has been fighting the inevitable closing of the black curtain. Don't feel guilty for this emotion. If you really did love the one who was in constant agony, then you should be grateful their pain is over. In all honesty, you were grieving already. You started when the first diagnosis came in, or when the emergency room called you. Your trip down that one-way Grief Street had already begun. The only thing you can do now is acknowledge it, accept it, and move on.

Another grief I'm familiar with is the non-death type. I'm talking about relationship grief. Some may say it's nothing but a huge disappointment, but others may agree it's a loss, a sort of death in the way it hits us. We're all human and people change throughout their lives. Change is normal and expected. People come into our lives, stay a while, then leave. We sometimes keep in touch with Christmas cards, or maybe a "like" on a social media post. People grow apart and that's as natural as anything under the sun. The relationship grief I'm talking about is the death of a bond you expected to last forever. There are people in your orbit you just KNOW will always be a part of your life. Come hell or high water, you know they'll always be there for you to call, visit, or count on in a crunch. Then the Universe throws you a curve and something happens. You have a fight, feelings are hurt, money matters trickle in, and so on. Perhaps old feelings of insecurity and jealousy finally raise their ugly heads and the hammer drops. Ties we once thought we'd have forever are suddenly severed, never to be reattached. I've been talking to numerous friends and acquaintances lately and I've come to realize everyone, without exception, has experienced some degree of relationship grief. The more I chat with these people, the more I realize how much we all have in common. The hurt is real. It's not just a pissing match between siblings or neighbors. It's not just a spat between friends that a cold beer or two will fix. When someone slices you to the core with no remorse whatsoever, the only thing you can do is walk away. If you've been cut free and pushed away emotionally, physically, and spiritually from someone, do yourself a favor and accept it as quickly as you can. Personally, I'm guilty of trying to bandage the wound, only to end up getting hurt further. Hard lesson, but sometimes the only choice to make is to nod your head and get moving. A wonderfully wise older woman once asked me, "If one of your friends was going through what you're going through right now, what would you tell her?"

I answered, "I'd tell her she's worth more than that. I'd say she doesn't deserve that sort of treatment." My wise friend nodded at me and asked me if I'm a good friend to myself? Oh, clever.

No matter what kind of grief we're feeling, it's all real. Everything you feel in your heart is true. If you're hurting, don't let anyone else tell you it's not pain. Ignore those who will tell you to just get over it, get on with your life. Yes, you will learn to deal with it, but you may never get over it. You will get on with your life, but you'll be forever changed as a person. Certain dates will trigger you. Birthdays, anniversaries, dates of an actual death will bitch slap you. Foods, smells, locations, and music will tug at your heart, and you'll be flooded with grief all over again. Your faith in others may waver now. Trust might be a hard thing to do with anyone new. You'll have scars and be battle weary. And all of this means you dared to love another human being. You opened yourself up to the possibility of being loved but also to the possibility of being hurt. There's that balance thing again. If you never take any chances, are you really living? Life isn't meant to be wrapped up in a pretty little package with a perfect bow on top. Life gets messy. Relationships last . . . or they don't. If they can be fixed, fix them. Don't let stubborn pride stand in your way, especially if the other person is trying to meet you halfway. Don't let selfish people hold you back from being happy. However, if there's absolutely no way a relationship can be salvaged, treat it like an actual death. Hold the hurt for a little while. Acknowledge it, feel it, then release it. It's not doing you any good to continue the years you have left mired in grief.

Grief. We will all deal with it in one form or another. The only comfort or solace I can comprehend where grief is concerned is this: the amount of pain you feel is only a fraction of the love you felt. The greatest love creates the greatest grief, but I believe it's still worth it.

JUST A PEEK

"We'll take just a peek. Just a quick peek and we'll be out of here." Those were the words my mother would utter right before we'd check out a house or building that was supposed to be haunted or have strange happenings occurring in them. I'll say this much for Marilyn C. King (Mickey), she had chutzpah. She knew damn well she was trespassing on these old condemned or abandoned properties. She also knew she possessed the innocent look and demeanor of any middle-aged Caucasian woman in northern New York. To say she used her mediocre housewife persona to her advantage would be a gross understatement. More on that later.

Mickey's only intention was to wander through these properties to see if they really were spooky, inhabited by spirits, or, as a total letdown, just empty spaces with no personality or character whatsoever. Mickey didn't engage in her criminal trespassing habit in the hopes of stealing or damaging anything. Graffiti never entered her mind, although she did dabble in acrylics on canvas now and then. What she was after was the intangible yet exciting possibility of communing with the spirits.

People would come to our house to have my mother read their cards. Now and then, someone would tell her about a particular structure, usually an old, empty house, that was supposedly haunted. She'd listen attentively to the stories these guests would tell and ask a multitude of questions. These people knew there was a pretty good chance Mickey would eventually take a trip to the aforementioned haunted abode and report back any findings. She definitely could have had her own show if ghost hunting had been popular back in the 1970's.

This particular story happened on October 2, 1978. I can tell you that precise date even without looking at my notes. I was in my senior year of high school, and the only other kid at home was my younger brother, Tim. It was the day before my parents' wedding anniversary. That afternoon, around 5:00 p.m., my mother watched my father and brother head out to the barn for the evening chores. She'd been a little antsy that day, but I had no idea why. Finally, once the door was closed and the guys were heading down the driveway, Mickey looked at me and asked, "Feel like a field trip?" The mischief in her eyes made me laugh and I gave her a big nod. She went into her bedroom closet and grabbed a small duffel bag and came back out to the kitchen.

"Change into some jeans and get your sneakers on," she suggested. To me, this meant we'd be someplace chilly, or perhaps in the woods, or anywhere that my legs could get scratched. She loved giving me just enough hints without really telling me what was going on. She could have written screenplays for the Mystery Channel.

Dressed in jeans, sneakers, and a dark hoodie, I joined Mickey in the old faded yellow Mercury Marquis sitting in the driveway. And down the road she drove. We headed toward a little hamlet called Bombay. On the car seat between us was the crude map she'd drawn from the notes she'd taken while visiting with her friend. After a number of turns off the main roads onto one-lane roads, then eventually to a dirt road, we were finally at our destination. I looked at her and made a *Deliverance* banjo joke. She quietly chuckled and aimed the Mercury into the weed-covered driveway. She pulled around to the rear of the house and backed it into the brambles as if preparing for a quick escape. This wasn't her first go 'round.

Mickey reached into the back seat and retrieved her small, worn duffel bag and said, "Let's go! We're burning daylight!" We giggled and exited the safe confines of the car and headed toward the dilapidated back porch. She made a comment about how still the air was, how there wasn't any wind that day. We stepped onto the porch and noticed the roof was hanging down about four feet lower on the left side than on the right. The screen door was askew as if it had seen too many Florida hurricanes. The inside door obviously had its share of children slamming it shut, as it was hanging precariously from the middle and bottom hinges. Mickey unzipped her bag and reached inside for a couple of small glass bottles. They looked like salt and pepper shakers, but without the holes on the top. Mickey unscrewed one of them and sprinkled some salt on the doorway where we would enter. On top of the salt, she shook the other container which I knew contained powdered sage. She used to say, "One can never be too careful." She then cautiously pushed the dangling door enough to wheedle her body into the kitchen.

I dutifully followed my fearless leader into the unknown. Her eyes met mine and she smiled. "You can feel it already, can't you?" she asked. I raised an eyebrow and smiled back. At that moment, we heard what sounded like a piece of furniture being dropped. The sound came from upstairs. My mother hollered out, "Hello? Is anyone in here?" No reply.

Our plan was to walk through each room of the house to make sure we weren't disturbing anyone or anything. Sometimes furry varmints like to hang out in these abandoned buildings and if you're not aware of their presence, they can scare the bejeebers out of you. We'd never run into any humans, so we considered it a bonus when we were the only living beings in a dwelling. We didn't see any food wrappers or sleeping bags. No signs of anyone bunking down for the night. From the large eat-in kitchen we tiptoed through the dining room, turned left and found a small living room. Again, we heard what sounded like something being dropped upstairs. The stairway leading up to the bedrooms was in the corner of the living room, so we gently placed our feet on each of the creaking stairs as we made our way to the second floor. Up there we found two small bedrooms and two that were pretty good sized. Surprisingly, none of the windows were broken in this house. That seemed odd, but it made our excursion easier because of what my mother did next.

In one of the bigger bedrooms was an old, battered chair that had seen its better days. It was laying on its side. That's when Mickey noticed the four dots on the floor where there wasn't any dust. Had this chair just been knocked over? Is that what we'd heard moments before? Mickey righted the chair, set her bag on it, and pawed through its contents. She finally pulled out a pack of wooden matches. "We'll start with the simple stuff," she said and proceeded to start talking to whatever or whomever might be in the house.

"Good afternoon," she said to thin air. "I'm Mickey and this is my daughter Pendra. We're not here to do any harm. We're just here to visit you." Her voice was steady and calm, not hurried or high-pitched at all. You'd swear she was the Avon lady about to show you the new fall colors in lipsticks. "I'm going to carefully light this match. If you'd care to make your presence known, please let me know through the flame."

And then she proceeded to light the wooden match. The smell of sulfur lingered in the air between us for a few seconds. She held the match between her thumb and forefinger in a vertical position. Nothing happened. The match burned down slowly, and when it came close to her fingers, she blew it out and reached into her bag for a glass jar with a lid. She tossed the burnt match into the jar and set it on the floor. Again, she lit another match. Same thing: saying hello to any spirits that may be there. This time, the match went out quickly. It hadn't even burned one-fourth of the way toward her fingertip. My mother's eyes looked over at mine and then she started smiling. That match went into the jar. A white candle was pulled out of the bag and lit. "We're just here to see if anyone is present. We don't want anything more than confirmation you're here." We waited. The candle flame started flickering, but stayed lit. We slowly walked through the rest of the bedrooms and the flame danced in different directions in each room. In one of the smaller rooms, the flame went sideways, almost as if it was pointing toward the tiny closet in that room. Mickey nodded to me then to the closet door. She passed a flashlight to me as, by this time, daylight was waning. I clicked the flashlight on, and reached for the closet door.

The old porcelain knob felt warm to the touch. It was almost as if someone had been standing there with a hand on the knob for a few minutes. Since it was early October, it was cool, but not super cold yet. Certainly, it was not hot or even comfortably warm in the house. I pulled my hand away for a second then looked around at my mother. "The doorknob is warm. The sunshine wouldn't have hit it in this direction." I was confused, but not alarmed. I reached for the doorknob again and, yes, it was still very warm to the touch. I opened the closet door and peered inside with the flashlight. Two bent wire hangers hung tiredly on the old metal pole that was used for a rod. There was nothing on the shelf, nothing on the floor. Just an empty closet. I was about to close the door when something caught my eye. I stepped inside the closet, turned around and aimed the beam of light on the inside door frame. There, about three feet from the floor, caught in the door frame was a small picture. It was of a little girl and, from the clothing and hair style, I'd guess the picture had been taken long ago. It was in black and white and slightly hazy. I pulled it out and handed it to my mother. Then we heard the chair in the other room again. Mickey just nodded at me and said, "Leave the picture." I tucked the picture back into the door frame and closed the closet door.

That small bedroom seemed to have a particularly strong, heavy feeling to it. Breathing seemed more labored in there, almost like how it feels to breathe on a hot, humid summer day. We made our way back to the chair. It was flipped over onto its side again, and closer to the window than it had been. Perhaps we were being too much of a nuisance to the occupants of the house. We left the upstairs bedrooms and headed back downstairs. The living room seemed empty, but not just of furniture and people. It seemed hollow in its soul. The dining room made the candle flame dance a little bit, but not as much as that bedroom. We walked slowly into the kitchen and the candle's flame started twitching. We looked for a draft but found none. We shielded the candle with our bodies, but it still jumped to the right and left. Finally, it was leaning toward the right, so we walked in that direction. We had totally missed a sliding door in the kitchen. I reached out and slid it to one side, revealing rickety old stairs to the basement. My mother stood at the top of the stairs and, before she could say or do anything, the candle's flame went out. There was no breeze or draft coming up from the cellar. Just putrid air from a dirt floor and damp basement. My mother gave an involuntary shiver and said, "That's enough. It's time to go."

She tucked everything into her duffel bag, and we carefully exited the house. Once we were outside, we both started inhaling deeply. The house didn't stink, per se, but it had a heaviness to it. We kicked our way through the scrub brush and picker bushes and let ourselves into the car. Mickey started it up and just as we were pulling out of the driveway onto the dirt road, a sheriff's patrol car was coming at us. "That was a pretty close call," Mickey said as she grinned at me. Hmmm . . . too close, I'd say because that sheriff turned around in the driveway and pulled us over. Damn. "Do you think Oscar will come visit me in jail for our anniversary tomorrow?" she joked.

"License, registration, and proof of insurance, please," demanded the uniformed gentleman. My mother produced all the requested paperwork. After a few minutes, which seemed like hours, the deputy came back and asked my mother what we were doing at that old house.

"Sir, we were looking for the Debyah farm and got all turned around." She waved her crudely drawn map briefly in front of the man then put it back on the car seat. "I'm just awful at directions. I pulled into that driveway to check my map, but I'm totally lost. Can you help me?" Her baby blue eyes shone with total innocence.

The sheriff had already glanced in our back seat and found

nothing unusual. No obviously stolen items, no kidnapped children, no bales of drugs.

"Ma'am, you must have missed the first left-hand turn by the big red barn up here. You're really close, just one road away."

"Oh! Thank you SO much, officer! I'm glad I didn't get too far out of the way!"

"You're welcome, ma'am. Might want to put a road map of the county in your glove box for future trips. Have a good day, ma'am."

"Great idea! Thanks again. You have a good day, too!" And with their good-byes said, my mother turned to me and smirked. Unbelievable.

A couple of weeks later, that same woman who had told my mother about the house near Bombay came for a visit. She couldn't wait to hear if Mickey had gone to that house or not, and when she was told yes, she could barely contain her excitement. Mickey asked this guest if there was anything she'd left out of her initial information concerning this particular haunted house. That's when she bit her lip and admitted that, yeah, she'd heard from her grandmother that a little girl had fallen down the cellar stairs and cracked her head on the stone wall of the foundation. The little girl died in that house and doesn't want people to forget she is still there. Then my mother went on to tell her guest about the flames, the picture in the closet, and that awful, dreadful feeling as she stood in the opened cellar doorway. The woman's eyes went wide. She was speechless. The stories she'd heard were true. That's all she wanted to know.

I drove by that house about twenty or so years ago. It's pretty much flattened out and the weeds and brush have taken over. Small trees have sprouted up in the driveway and the original trees have fallen over and are rotting where they landed. I pulled off the road slightly and got out of my car. As I carried a small bag toward what was left of this carcass of a house, I swear I could feel someone watching me. I didn't feel threatened or worried. Just aware. I reached the front corner of the house and pulled a small doll out of the bag I was carrying. I placed it on a piece of rotting wood and said, "Just in case you're still here . . ." I walked back to my car and as I was opening the door, I thought, for just a split second, that I heard a little girl giggle.

STUFF IT!

I'll go out on a limb here and say most of you reading this essay had, or still have, stuffed animals from your childhood. Our parents, grandparents, godparents, aunts, uncles, and anyone who gave us the googly eyes when we were born, gifted us with these soft companions. As children we were encouraged to love them, take care of them, and talk to them as if they were our real friends.

"Isn't it cute that Little Johnny talks to his teddy bear?" "Isn't it adorable how Sally covers her bunny with a blanket?" We're taught to use our imaginations as children. It's fine to pretend our faithful companions can hear and understand us, and sometimes even reply to us. Nobody sees anything wrong with it until . . . it happens. There's some age that is kept top secret from all of us. But it's there. There's an age when we're supposed to put our "toys" away and never talk to them again. We're told to GROW UP. We hear those fateful words: ACT YOUR AGE. Confusing, isn't it? After all, being conditioned, or dare I say trained, from birth to love and adore our inanimate critters is considered normal. Then we're abruptly told we must turn our backs on our ever-loyal friends because a certain number has been reached on our biological calendar. How unfair is that?

Fortunately, there are a few of us, nay, MORE than a few of us, who are openly defiant of this forced "rule." I recently joined a group on social media that loves and cherishes everything about Bill Watterson's comic strip *Calvin and Hobbes*. I was a mere 24 years old when the brilliant Bill Watterson created this comic strip back in 1985. It's about a little six-year-old boy named

Calvin and his stuffed tiger, Hobbes. Hobbes is seen through the eyes of Calvin most of the time. And in those moments, he's alive. Hobbes is as real as any human you've ever met. He and Calvin go on adventures, get into trouble, and ponder the universe. Watterson hit the nail on the head. To those of us who have had the privilege of a stuffed companion, this comic strip was more than entertainment. It was taking us back in time and letting us relive our younger years. How many times did we play pirates? How often did we dread school because we had procrastinated finishing a project due that particular day? Was bath time a pain in the butt until we actually hopped into that stormy sea of foamy bubbles? Watterson lets us live again as children through the eyes of Calvin and Hobbes.

When I was a child, I had a couple of stuffed animals. I didn't have a whole zoo or enough to fill a huge net suspended from the ceiling like some kids, but I had a couple I loved with all my heart. I think that's the key–to have only a couple because then you can truly love them. If you have three dozen stuffed animals, how will you ever love them all equally? How can you get to them all every day? You can't. Someone's going to feel left out and ignored. I had a teddy bear and, later, a dog. My two guardians slept with me every night. I carried the teddy bear in the crook of my arm when I was hanging around the house. My dog was excellent at helping me watch cartoons on Saturday morning and Disney on Sunday nights. I never took them with me if I left the house. I think I was afraid I'd lose my companions, or they'd get hurt somehow and I just couldn't stomach the thought of either of those things happening to my best friends. I've been clocking in for six decades and, yes, I still have those two friends. The teddy bear sits on a high shelf in my bedroom where he's safe from any visitors with dogs who like to tear up what they see as fair game. He has a few bald spots where he's been repeatedly hugged and loved throughout the years. He doesn't seem to mind. The dog is in such fragile condition from years of squeezing that he now resides in a see-through box on the top shelf of my closet. Being close to sixty years old has been tough on the old boy. I'm sure he prefers the safety and security of his enclosed perch.

And then there's one more. A tiger. This one is relatively recent. He's only about fifteen years or so old. I can't remember exactly when I received him and, if I'm honest, I think he was a bit of a mocking gift at that. The person who gave him to me knew I was a huge fan of *Calvin and Hobbes*. As a matter of fact, she knew I had adopted two kittens from the family farm in 1986 and had named them Calvin and Hobbes. Unfortunately, poor little Calvin the kitten was sickly when I brought the two of them home. My vet tried to save him but, sadly, Calvin died. However, I had Hobbes for sixteen years. Much like Watterson's Calvin, I loved my friend Hobbes wholeheartedly. He and I went through numerous ups and downs. He saw me through job changes, different boyfriends, subsequent heartaches, and the rest of what life threw at me. Hobbes was my sounding board. He never judged me. His only purpose in life was to comfort me and be my constant companion. He did an excellent job his entire sixteen years. I totally comprehended six-year-old Calvin's logic. Whether it's a stuffed animal or a real one, they understand and love us unconditionally.

I didn't name my current stuffed tiger Hobbes. I couldn't do it. I'd already been blessed with a Hobbes in my life and, although he'd been gone for a number of years, I just couldn't bring myself to use his name again. I knew I needed a different name for this stuffed tiger. The show NCIS was big at the time, and I liked the character Tony DiNozzo. And that's how DiNozzo came to be in my home. He's not Tony DiNozzo. Just . . . DiNozzo.

Here's an interesting thing about DiNozzo–he's well-traveled. I can't remember the first trip I took him on, but I started taking him on my jaunts. I'd post pictures of him at various locations and the comments I'd get were hilarious. Of course, I received the expected eye rolls from the people who were disgusted with me. After all, a woman in her 40's (at that time) carrying a stuffed toy with her? How silly is THAT? Guess what? The more I traveled with this tiger, the more laughs and

PENDRA J KING

smiles happened. Two of my friends still use DiNozzo's travels to teach their children geography and history. When I was in Rome doing the tourist thing, DiNozzo "taught" several children about the Colosseum, Trevi Fountain, and the catacombs. (Did I say CATacombs?) He's been through Germany and Austria. DiNozzo loves the Caribbean. Las Vegas gets him going every time. He's quite fond of Boothbay Harbor, Maine. He's also hit a few other New England states. He's been an excellent travel companion and isn't demanding at all. What's not to love? For years now I've looked at DiNozzo as my own version of Calvin's Hobbes. I still take him on trips with me now and, as superstitious as I am, I feel he's a good luck charm. Whenever he travels with me, I make all my connecting flights (some early), I sometimes get an upgraded seat on a plane, or I get a nicer room in a hotel than I had originally booked. He's made sure I've never had a flat tire, nor have I broken down on the highway. Coincidence? I think not. When we're not out and about, DiNozzo stays here at home. He sits on my living room sofa and is ready to listen whenever I want to bounce ideas off him. Once in a while I'll be upset about something and just need to vent. He's there to listen. More than once I've had crushing news and he's been silent, knowing there aren't any words to comfort me, but his presence is enough. On the other hand, I swear I can see him smile when I share happy news with him.

I'm curious to know how many of you still have your friends tucked away, hidden like an embarrassing secret, in the back of your closet? Perhaps it's time to dig them out and let them know you haven't forgotten them. If they're not on the verge of disintegration, do you have anyone special you can share them with now? Do you have children or grandchildren who will love and appreciate them? You know these friends have never stopped loving you. No matter how grown or mature you've become, they've never forsaken you or your time together all those years ago. They'll forgive you for cramming them into the hot attic. They'll let bygones be bygones when you haul that damp trunk up from the cellar. One look at their faces will let you know this. If you have nobody to share your faithful companions with, why not enjoy them again for yourself? Can't you find a spot on your dresser for your bear? Isn't there room on the bookshelf for your version of Hobbes?

For some reason, loving an inanimate object angers certain people. As I mentioned at the beginning of this essay, when we're young we're encouraged to love and confide in our stuffed animals. We're told to find comfort in them. Why does this need to stop because our bodies have aged? Why must we deny ourselves solace from any pain the world has dished out to us? Are we hurting anyone? No. Are we depriving others of food, air, or shelter? No. They're angry at us because we're allowing our inner child to have a voice, even if it's only for a moment. It's what they want but are too grown up and mature to do. Now, I admit there are a few people out there who may be just a little over the line. These people can't function on a normal level. These folks need special help dealing with reality and I certainly hope they're getting it. There's a difference between having a healthy imagination and being totally out of touch with reality. It may be a fine line, but it's there. I've always been able to function properly, even with my highly active imagination. I've always held a job, my bills have been paid on time, I bathe every day, and I don't live in a "reality tv" hoarder's home. I have healthy relationships with my friends and neighbors. I socialize with real human beings, love real animals, and know the earth is not flat. (I'm still hoping Elvis is alive, but I'm becoming a little more disheartened every day.) So, yes, I'm fine. I'm not flipping out or out of touch with reality. I'm just enjoying being a kid now and then.

I figure when I croak and get cremated (hopefully at least 20 years from now), my bear and dog will be almost dust by then, so I'd like them toasted at the same time. Yes, I'm selfish enough to want to take them with me. I've even made it known that when I die, DiNozzo is to go to a young friend and she's to take him with her when she travels. She was honored to be named as his companion when the time comes. (Thank you, Sici

Kahrs!)

    I still chuckle when I get the side-eye or when someone actually says something snarky to me about DiNozzo. These are the same people who carry their good luck charms or who have to wear a certain piece of jewelry for protection from all harm. They mock me for my imagination but can't see their own hypocrisy. To those people I have one thing to say: STUFF IT!

HOW BAD?

Ahh, Netflix. You bewitch me. Once again, I'm on another streak where I tend to gravitate toward a certain kind of movie. Most of the time I like to mix it up with romcoms, action, mysteries, and so on. For some reason lately I've been leaning toward the darker, more psychological thrillers. A few of them have pretty much the same theme: How bad could you be? How mean, cruel, or angry could you get if provoked? Most of these movies involve a parent (usually a retired Special Forces dad) going after the bad guys who kidnapped his child. Now and then, it's a mom who has to do some pretty gnarly stuff to get her kid back in one piece or to get a sibling out of a mess with drug lords.

These movies make me sit and ponder: How bad could I ever get? What lines am I willing to cross for loved ones? For myself? Would I cross those same lines for a total stranger? If that stranger is a bad person, would I still value his/her life enough to risk my own? What is a life worth to me? Is my life any more valuable than the next person's? Or are we all equal on this ride called life?

Hollywood gives us an outlet. The movie industry lets us live out our primitive instincts without ever getting hurt or called into action in real life. We watch those macho men and women mop the floor with the bad guys. We smile when the villain gets blown away or falls twenty stories and splatters onto a deserted sidewalk. It's a lot like those pretend soldier video/computer games that are so popular today. We can sit in the comfort of our cozy chairs and annihilate the enemy without a second thought. There are no consequences, no guilt, shame, or need to justify our actions. If we get blown up, no worries! We'll just come back in the next round. Then we can wander out to the kitchen, crack open another cold beverage, and go back to slaying those dragons or people. Whatever your imagination and the screen show you are what you can conquer. I'm sure some people have been in situations where they've had to tussle with another person, whether it be by profession, or by chance. If you've chosen a profession where physical altercations are the norm, would you grow insensitive to violence after a while? Would fighting become part of your routine? Golly, I guess I'll brush my teeth, take out the trash, mow the lawn, then kick someone's butt today. Does violence become a way of life for some? Does it become, dare I say, almost like an addictive drug? Do we feel the need to play these video games or watch these tough guy movies as a way to get our fix? Or is it our minds just letting us act out what our instincts tell us to do?

Personally, I believe we all have that killer instinct in us. How else would we have survived all these years? Now that we don't have to fight the saber tooth tiger to live another day, do we still have that fight or flight instinct? Yes. And that's why these movies and games appeal to us. I think deep down we want to know we COULD fight if called upon to do so. We live vicariously through these characters on our screens. We don't really WANT to get punched, kicked, stabbed, or whatever because, damn, that hurts! Still, knowing you could defend yourself is a fantastic feeling.

Back to my original thought: How bad could you be? I've asked myself this question many times while watching my favorite high body count movies. I connect with the good guys who are seeking vengeance. I cheer for the ones who are the underdogs, beaten within an inch of their lives and yet they dig deep and find the strength to kick ass and take names. Would I ever be that tough? Could I find the guts to hold strong and defend myself or those close to me? I'd like to think so. I can take verbal criticism, but if it came down to a physical altercation, would I be brave enough to give it my all?

Yes.

I refuse to be a victim. I abhor the helpless female who cowers and waits for her rescuer to arrive. It may not be pretty or graceful, but I won't go down without a fight. I've always been a lover, not a fighter. Oh sure, I've had some throwdowns with my siblings, but hey, that's expected in a large family. Still, I've never loved violence for the sake of violence. You all know I'm the biggest Rocky Balboa fan out there, but it's not for boxing. I don't like fighting. It's all the other great life lessons the Rocky series offers that make me love that character so much. And yet, I holler and punch the air as Rocky beats the bejeebers out of Apollo Creed, Clubber Lang, and Ivan Drago. (We can all pretend *Rocky V* and Tommy Gunn didn't happen, okay?)

As humans, we may shun violence on the surface, but below our skin lies an animal. We have animal instincts, and those instincts tell us to protect ourselves and those closest to us. I'm willing to bet if the shit hits the fan, I'll be unrecognizable. This older woman will turn into your worst nightmare if provoked. I don't claim to be a tough mothertrucker, but if backed into a corner, you can bet your last dime I'll come out swinging. I won't crumble until my last ounce of strength and courage have been spent. I will definitely defend myself and those around me with every fiber of my body and soul.

You can bet your life on that.

MANLY MEN

As you know, I love to people-watch. It's been a hobby since I was a kid. Maybe I watched too many spy movies as a child. James Bond has always been a staple in my life. Then all those detective shows popped up and I was right there with Columbo, Rockford, Kojak, and McCloud. I fell instantly in love with San Francisco's Inspector Harry Callahan. It wasn't always because the lead character was handsome and dapper. I can honestly say Columbo and Kojak never made my tiddly wink. What I was drawn to was their intelligence, character, wit, and ability to see people and situations outside their normal realms. They people-watched and picked up on subtle clues. I realize all the credit goes to the writers of these shows, but they made their characters believable and, dare I say, lovable. We were shown how brilliant, masculine, and tough these guys were. Once in a while we were treated to their softer side. We'd see them vulnerable or broken–so human. It didn't happen often, because these guys were manly men. This is where I learned what the expression "he's a man's man" meant. And I liked it. I'll openly admit I like manly men. I love manly men. Give me war heroes, cowboys, and construction workers. Add in some farmers, hunters, and fishermen. (Please keep in mind, this essay is coming from a heterosexual female and I'm talking about my observances on heterosexual males only. Thank you.) I'm not a fan of today's soft boys who have grown into soft men. This is what I've noticed in the past twenty or so years of people-watching. Our manly men are becoming extinct. I may be showing my backwoods, redneck, not-yet-evolved female mind, but I'll let you in on a secret: I'm not alone.

Let me back it up for just a second. I'm NOT a fan of abusers, control freaks, or narcissistic idiots. I've never been a "me Tarzan, you Jane" type of woman. I was raised to work hard, support myself, and to never mooch off anyone, especially a man. Men who are brash, too cocky, or rude don't get my vote. In my opinion, men who are like that are showing their insecurities, fears, and self-doubts. A confident man doesn't need to dominate or belittle a woman. There has to be a happy medium somewhere between these macho jerks and today's wimpy girly boys.

Now, before all you women's libbers jump on me, just hold up for a second. I'm all about equal rights, respect, and women being able to do the same jobs as men. Hell, I had a job that was predominately male-run. I understand we can do most things men can and that's wonderful. This essay isn't about that. This isn't about equal rights and proving we're just as tough as the men out there. I'm not saying we should be little pansy-ass bitches who can't do anything for ourselves, either. What I'm writing about is MEN, so leave your egos at the door for a minute, please.

I took an informal poll with a bunch of women I know. They were of all ages, starting in their early 20's and way into their 70's. Without fail, each and every one of them expressed a preference for a manly man, not a girly boy. Is this basic instinct in females? Is it all about breeding and ensuring the future of our species? Maybe. What about those of us who have no desire to reproduce? Surprise, surprise! We still prefer manly men over sissy boys. We don't care about adding to the world's population, so that's not it. We're just naturally drawn to the more attractive dominant traits of yesterday's men.

When I see a man wearing an old denim or flannel shirt with the sleeves rolled up, I smile. If he has callouses on his hands or dirt under his fingernails, that's not a bad thing. I don't mind worn out jeans or even ones with a rip or two, but only if they were ripped by accident and not bought from a store that way. Right now, it's prime hunting season and I watch the pickup trucks go by my house in the wee hours of the morning. These guys are heading out in the brisk fall air to trudge across frost-laden fields to get to their favorite hunting spots. They'll wait quietly for hours for the chance to shoot a deer, thus feeding themselves and their loved ones. Call me old fashioned, but I admire this. Men who can hammer a nail, fix machinery, plumb a house, or install safe electrical systems are tops in my book. Here's a huge shout-out to the roofers and concrete workers. My heart jumps when I see a lineman climbing a pole while wearing his heavy tool belt. The Chippendales dancers dress in cowboy outfits or construction worker clothing for a reason. Pocket protectors and video game controls just don't do it for us.

Back to manly men. The expression "toxic masculinity" ticks me off. If a man dares to open a door for a woman, he's labeled as toxic. What the HELL? Good manners, respect, and courtesy are toxic? PUH-LEASE! Why are we trying to neuter gentlemen? Now, if a stranger holds the door open for you, then slaps your booty on your way through then, yes, that's toxic; however, if a man is being kind and wants to treat you with respect, let him. Enjoy it. Thank him. There's a huge difference between chivalry and chauvinism. Being attractive means different things to different people. I'm just writing about my own preferences here so if you agree with my way of thinking, welcome to the club. If you don't, and you prefer today's tender, delicate, "I'll hire it done" guys, then more power to you. You're not taking anything I want, so you're more than welcome to your choice, just as I am to mine.

When did this softening of our men begin? Where did we change course and turn our backs on manly men? What went wrong? What's so awful about men who are strong and capable? Like so many other topics, I feel we've taken it too far. Society has over-corrected when it comes to men. The chauvinistic days of the Mad Men mentality are over. Movies and television shows portraying men as the only ones whose opinions matter are fading out and I'm glad to see them go. I have total respect for the men who don't buy into that macho attitude anymore. Teaching our little boys to be more understanding, kind, polite, and tolerant is great. Still, I don't believe castrating all men for the sake of bringing them down is the answer. I don't want to live in a society full of mommy's boys. I can't imagine all the men out there being just as feminine or even more feminine than women. Too many young men these days haven't learned what their fathers know. Skills that should be passed down to their sons (and daughters) are being abandoned. WHY? Because it's easier to let them play video games than to get them off their butts and out to the woods. These dainty metrosexual lads just don't cut it for me. A guy in skinny jeans and hair gel isn't attractive to me. Give me a real man. Give me a man with callouses on his hands, not his ass. I have no problem with his well-worn work boots sitting on the floor under his faded Wrangler jeans. Show me a man whose toolbox is in disarray from constant use. Let me see those hunting magazines in his bathroom and deer heads on the wall of his man cave. I'll happily get out of his way when he's wielding a shovel or operating a backhoe.

There you have it. I love manly men and I won't apologize for it.

For any of you men out there reading this: Please continue to be real men. For the love of all that is holy, don't let society neuter you. Even if they won't always openly admit it, the majority of women out there LOVE manly men. I am not alone. I'm in good company. Keep hunting, fishing, building, plowing, fixing, and creating. Get dirty. Get scruffy. We know you clean up well and we appreciate it but, damn, when you walk in all dusty and spent, you're oozing that yummy masculinity and we love it. To us, it's not toxic. It's delicious.

MY UNCLE LEE

I could kick myself in the ass for not paying closer attention to certain people in my life. Now they're gone and I can't ask any more questions. I can't hear their stories over and over again. At the time, I'd roll my eyes and think to myself, *here we go again*, and be bored out of my mind when one of the old folks would tell the same story AGAIN. Oh, what I wouldn't give now to sit down with these people and soak up all their wit and wisdom! One in particular who I miss is my Uncle Lee.

My uncle Lee was 15 years older than my mother. He was born in 1921 but had a rough beginning. He was conceived out of wedlock, and back in those days it was a huge sin. If anyone bothered to do the math on most of the firstborns back then, they'd shut their righteous traps, wouldn't they? My grandparents had a quick wedding, and Uncle Lee was born a healthy, full-term bouncing baby boy seven months later. When he was old enough to go to school, some of the other children decided they'd teach him a lesson for being a bastard child. As if it was his fault for his parents having sex before marriage? I guess so. On his way home from school one day, several older children jumped six-year-old Lee and proceeded to tar and feather him. The slathered thick, black, sticky tar all over his body, including his hair and face. They threw feathers on him and kicked him around on the ground until he was covered. All the while, these children were screaming, "BASTARD! BASTARD! LEE IS A BASTARD!" When they figured they'd taught him a good lesson, they left him alone on the ground, barely able to move. He somehow made his way back home. When his parents saw him, they were embarrassed. They were angry at the children who did this to Lee, but they were more embarrassed that everyone knew Lee was what others sneeringly called a "ten-pound preemie." That was the derogatory term for any child who came sooner than nine months after a wedding. Instead of showing more compassion for their child who was ridiculed and tortured for something over which he had no control, they shipped him off to his grandparents. His grandparents were cold and cruel and obviously took child rearing lessons from old English literary novels such as *Oliver Twist*.

And yet, Uncle Lee did not break. He ended up graduating from high school with honors. He entered the military and served his country honorably. I still have a picture of him in his uniform. Let me put it this way, Frank Sinatra would have been jealous of Uncle Lee's blue eyes. And Elvis Presley would have been called ugly if he'd stood next to Uncle Lee. He eventually ended up as an electrician for Alcoa in Massena. I remember when my family used to live downstate in western New York and my mother and Uncle Lee would write letters back and forth on a regular basis. They both had manual typewriters, but they were special. They were script typewriters. In my little head, that was just the ultimate in typing. No plain ol' block lettering. This was cursive writing, but on a freakin' typewriter! And what made this correspondence even more special was how Uncle Lee sent his letters to my mother. His letters were always in business-sized manila envelopes with . . . wait for it . . . a WAX SEAL AND STAMP ON THE BACK! Oh my GOD! I had a sneaking suspicion my Uncle Lee was actually royalty. I'd seen movies in which the king sent letters or he wrote laws and decrees and everything was sealed with wax and a stamp. My uncle was a king. He lived far away and had special envelopes and wax seals. How much more evidence do you need? Years later, we moved up to the north country and I saw his little pink house on Roosevelt Street in Massena. I confess I was a little disappointed there was no moat around his house. Sigh. Oh well. I still loved him.

Uncle Lee used to sit at our kitchen table sucking down

cup after cup of coffee. He'd scoop three spoonfuls of sugar and a glug of fresh cream into each cup. He always stirred counterclockwise and tapped his spoon three times on the edge of his cup before placing it on his saucer. He'd pull out his pack of little cigarillos (they were the size of cigarettes, but were brown like cigars), and light one before he began each story.

I remember Uncle Lee would bring out the *New York Times* newspaper and sit down with us to do the crossword puzzle. He did the puzzle in pen. In. PEN. I swear I've never met anyone else who could do the NYT crossword in pen. Correctly, of course. He taught us so many words that we promptly forgot, but loved being our teacher for that half hour. To this day when I'm feeling utterly cocky I'll pick up a local newspaper and attempt to do the puzzle in pen. I fail every time and I hear the ghost of Uncle Lee snickering at me. I love it.

Uncle Lee was also a gifted artist. He loved to doodle and most of the time when he would visit the farm, he'd ask us to go grab a piece of paper and a pen. He'd have us draw a line or any squiggly shape on the paper. He'd then proceed to create a beautiful or hilarious picture for our enjoyment. I still have one of his drawings and I cherish it.

One of Uncle Lee's favorite stories was about when he was a tail gunner in World War Two. He described the plane in detail. The space where he sat at the bottom of the plane was cramped and cold. There was no room for his body to move around except for his arms and trigger finger. One day he was tucked into position ready to shoot down any enemies he could see. He'd been going for days without a break. It was a war. There were no time clocks to punch or scheduled breaks. And then he did the unthinkable: he nodded off. For one slight second, his chin hit his chest and he fell asleep. Just as quickly as he'd nodded off, he awoke and saw another airplane THIS CLOSE. With his finger on the trigger, he was half a breath away from shooting that other plane down when he saw something. He saw the co-pilot hand the pilot a cup of tea. Even in my uncle's sleep-deprived brain, he knew that only the English would stop in the middle of a dogfight to have a cup of tea. Uncle Lee's finger eased off the trigger and, in that moment, the other plane was gone. He never forgot how that cup of tea saved those two men that day.

Uncle Lee had many stories and now I wish he'd taken the time to write them all down. Trying to remember his tales frustrates me because I can't do them justice.

Another war story was when the plane he was in was flying so low that he could see the piles of bodies at the concentration camps. He didn't tell us about these horrors to scare us. He wanted us to know what Hitler did to all those innocent people. This was also his way of educating us to always stick up for those who can't fight for themselves. Uncle Lee vividly described the twisted, bloody bodies piled like firewood. Now and then he'd see an arm or hand moving, a human being still barely alive trying to crawl out from under the murdered innocents. Uncle Lee's face was pained, and his eyes would get slightly wet, but he held it together. The crimes against humanity that man saw stayed with him forever. He only told a few horror stories, but that was purely for educational purposes, not to frighten us. He told us some history should never be repeated. He was right.

Uncle Lee had a decent job at Alcoa and only had one child who, by the time we moved up here, was an adult and out on his own. Uncle Lee's wife never liked coming to the farm because it was beneath her. She was a self-appointed important person who looked down on poor people. She and Uncle Lee weren't rich by any means, but they were certainly comfortable. Now and then he would come out to the farm with a box of ice cream. We'd all giggle and try our best to not tackle him when we saw a brown paper bag under his arm when he walked into the kitchen. My mother would roll her eyes at him and he'd just grin as he told us to grab the bowls and spoons. He knew the story about eating ice cream before noon, so he always made sure he showed up before 12:00 p.m. Uncle Lee would scoop out the delicious treat but before we could dive in, he'd look at us with a pseudo-serious face and make us hold up our right hand and swear we would not tell Aunt Betty about the ice cream. We all swore we'd take his secret to the grave with us. Uncle Lee loved making us co-conspirators.

Another thing I remember and loved about Uncle Lee was his Volkswagen bug. He had the first bug in this area (and for all I know, the ONLY one) outfitted with a Rolls Royce hood up front and a Lincoln Continental tire mold in the back. That was classic Uncle Lee. He was brilliant, yet whimsical. He loved that car and drove it whenever Aunt Betty wasn't with him. She would NOT be seen dead in that . . . that . . . THING! To her it was SO unclassy. To him, it was the ultimate toy.

Uncle Lee died in 1982. He was sitting at his typewriter at his dining room table when he keeled over and died from a heart attack at age 61, the same age I am now. I never found out to whom his last letter was addressed, and that will always remain a mystery. I remember his was the first funeral I'd ever attended. As I walked into the funeral home, I saw him laid out in the casket. I couldn't fathom how that wonderful man could be dead. He'd survived so much in his short life (by today's standards). I stared at his lifeless body in the box. I willed his chest to rise and fall with life's breath, but it didn't happen. Part of my world crumbled that day. Up until that moment, I'd only known death from second-hand stories from friends. I'd experienced the death of pets, but that loss far outweighed anything else I'd ever known or felt. My heart hurt. I couldn't comprehend a man of his caliber accepting death for himself. And yet, there he was. Still. Silent. The funeral was held, and we all shuffled out of the flower-filled room. It took me a while to come to grips with never seeing Uncle Lee again. His was the first real death I faced and, I have to say, he set the bar pretty high for all those who followed.

PARENTAL ODDS AND ENDS

Everyone has a moment or two (or many more in my case) etched into their minds of something silly or profound their parents have said or done. My parents were strict but loving. They also had a pretty warped sense of humor and I'm certain I inherited this trait from them. I tell people it's genetic. I didn't have a choice or a chance. In no particular order, I'll share a few odds and ends that have stayed with me all these years.

******

You've heard of larks and owls when it comes to people and their sleeping habits, right? My father was a lark, up at the crack of dawn to milk the cows. My mother, on the other hand, was an owl. She preferred to stay up late reading books or writing in her journals.

My mother would usually head to bed around midnight or 1:00 a.m. but before she headed off to slumber, she'd set up the big coffee pot for the morning. Mickey would fill the pot's reservoir with water, load the basket with coffee grounds, and place a cup nearby for my father.

Oscar was the early bird of the family. He rolled out of his comfy bed at 4:30 a.m. and quietly dressed before heading to the kitchen. He'd flip the button on the coffee pot and start the morning's brew. Oscar would sip a cup of coffee while getting his boots on, then head to the barn to start milking 40 cows.

This one particular morning Oscar came back into the

house after chores and poured himself another cup of coffee. Mickey was just getting up. She wandered into the kitchen bleary-eyed and reached into the cupboard for her favorite cup and poured herself a serving of that delicious ebony fluid. Mickey sat down at her end of the table and noticed Oscar looking at her with a puzzled look on his face. She cocked her head to one side and asked him what was on his mind.

"I don't mean to complain, but I think you made the coffee a little too strong this morning." Oscar tried to sound appreciative, but he needed to let her know something wasn't right. He then moved his hand away from his coffee cup and sticking straight out of the middle of his full cup of coffee was his spoon. "I tried to stir my sugar but it's just a little too thick and strong this morning. How many scoops of coffee grounds did you put in last night?"

My mother stared at his cup with the teaspoon sticking straight up in the middle of it, not even touching the sides. Her eyes went wide. She looked down at her own cup then back up at his. Her foggy morning mind couldn't comprehend what was happening. Finally, Oscar started chuckling and pulled the spoon up and that's when Mickey noticed he'd dug the bottom of his spoon into a small potato as an anchor. She shook her head and called him a colorful name. Then they both started laughing. I have yet to pull this on anyone, but I'm always on the lookout for an opportunity.

******

Another story about my mother is about ice cream. One day back in 1953, my newly married parents were living in Ithaca. My father was working as a herdsman at Cornell University. The folks didn't have any of us children at the time, so it was just the two of them in their little apartment. One Saturday, Oscar was in the kitchen at about 10:00 a.m. and he decided he wanted a little snack. He always had a sweet tooth, so he reached into the freezer and pulled out a carton of ice cream.

He scooped out a bowlful and put the carton back. He was about half-way finished eating his treat when my mother walked into the kitchen and freaked out.

"OSCAR! STOP! STOP!" Mickey was panicking, reaching for his bowl of ice cream. Oscar stopped eating thinking she was hurt or needed help immediately.

"What? What's wrong?" he asked, worry setting in fast.

"YOU CAN'T EAT THAT! IT'S NOT NOON! YOU CAN'T EAT THAT!"

Oscar looked down at his bowl, then back up at her. Ice cream? HUH? "What do you mean I can't eat this? I bought it. It's paid for. We're not saving it for any celebration, are we?" he asked, totally confused.

"Oscar," my mother said in exasperation, "you can't eat ice cream until noon or you'll get worms!"

He started laughing. He had to sit down and put his bowl on the table. "What on earth are you talking about, Mickey?"

"My parents told us we should never eat ice cream before noon, or we'll get worms. I don't want you to get worms. I'm just looking out for you."

Ahhh, so that explained it. My mother's family went through the Great Depression and World War II, so to say they had to be frugal was an understatement. Ice cream was an extremely rare treat for my mother and her siblings. Once in a blue moon they'd either make a batch or, if they had a special occasion, they'd get store-bought ice cream. My mother's parents didn't want the children to scarf down this frozen confection just because it was sitting in the freezer. It had to be a treat, and only in the evening after supper was served.

Once my mother explained where that gem of wisdom came from, Oscar sat her down and asked her to think about it. He said, "Mickey, tell me what exactly is going to change if I sit here for another two hours and THEN eat this same bowl of ice cream." Mickey thought about it. Embarrassment crept up into her face. She started to giggle, then laugh.

"Oh my God. How many other lies did my parents tell

me?" She shook her head at the thought. Then she went to the cupboard and pulled out a bowl for herself.

Speaking of stretching the truth, my father's parents had a few of their own. One that stayed with my father throughout his lifetime was the red suspenders. The three boys in the family always had red suspenders because, as his father told him, "Red suspenders will keep you warm in the winter." Whenever I see someone wearing red suspenders, I smile and think of my father wearing them as a young lad.

******

Another gag my father pulled on my unsuspecting mother was when he sent her to Guertin's Hardware store in Winthrop. The new Stewart's store is there now but back in 1974, it was a family-owned hardware store. Oscar was working around the house trying to get things squared away. He sent my mother to Guertin's for a left-handed stove pipe wrench. Without even thinking about it, off she went to Winthrop. She walked into the store and wandered the aisles looking for this particular wrench her husband needed. Finally giving up, she went to the counter and asked the owner if he could help her find what her husband wanted. "What is it exactly that your husband needs?" the owner asked.

"A left-handed stove pipe wrench," was my mother's reply.

The store owner smiled a little. "Who's your husband, ma'am?" he asked.

"Oscar King. Why? Why does it matter who wants it?" My mother was getting a bit perturbed at this point.

Smiling, the owner just said, "Ma'am, I know Oscar. He's quite the character. There's no such thing as a left-handed stove pipe wrench. As a matter of fact, you don't really use wrenches on stove pipes, you just slide and tap them into place." He was trying to keep his face straight, but he wasn't succeeding.

My mother was seething. She drove home in the old station wagon contemplating all the ways she could kill her husband and get rid of the body. It wasn't a pretty sight when she walked through the door and saw Oscar sitting at the kitchen table. I'll just leave it at that.

******

Another time Oscar pulled a good one was at the local Agway store in Winthrop. Baker Elliott and Bun Francis knew him as a regular customer and often waited for whatever joke he was going to tell next. Oscar went in one day when he saw a new lady was working at the counter. Turns out she was Baker's daughter, Cindy. He casually walked up and asked if his post holes were in yet? Cindy Elliott was just learning the ropes, so she looked to the older gentlemen who had been there for ages and asked where she could find out if specific orders had arrived at the store. They showed her a special logbook for orders and let her peruse the list of customers and their requests. That poor gal went through the list several times looking for Oscar King's post holes. The guys behind the counter looked at Oscar and grinned, knowing this was going to be a good one. "I ordered them three weeks ago," Oscar said. "It's fencing season, and I have to get all my fence posts in before I let the cows out of the barn for spring." She kept looking. No fence post holes order to be found. Someone screwed up. Or maybe she just didn't know what to look for in the special orders book. Cindy went all over the store looking for Oscar's order. In her mind, she was thinking "fence post hole digger" and not just the holes. Finally, she turned to Oscar and said, "I'm sorry, but I just can't find your order. Could it be under someone else's name?"

Oscar started smirking. The gentlemen behind the counter couldn't hold it in any longer and they started laughing.

Finally, Oscar was introduced to Cindy, and she was warned that he was a joker. Then Baker asked her to say aloud what Oscar had supposedly ordered. "Post holes," was her reply. He told her to say it again. "Post holes . . . OH MY GOD!!!" The light went on in her head. Then all of them started laughing and Cindy said she'd be keeping an eye out for Oscar in the future. Some of Oscar's fondest memories are from the Agway store in Winthrop. When I told Cindy I'd like to include this story in my next book, she wholeheartedly agreed to share it. Then she reminded me of another little goodie Oscar used to pull on his unsuspecting victims.

******

Oscar had somehow gotten his hands on a glass eye. They aren't like in the movies. They aren't round like marbles. Only one half is round, the part someone would see if they were looking at the person wearing it. The other side is a little bit concave. Oscar used to slip the glass eye into his mouth and place his tongue in the groove in the back of the eyeball. He'd part his lips slightly and slip the eye back and forth as if it was looking around. He used to tell people he was checking out the ladies with that eye. It was terribly freaky yet hilarious at the same time.

Thank you, Cindy and your daughter Brigitte Niles Snell, for the details on the Oscar-Agway stories.

BRASHER'S MOST HAUNTED CEMETERY

"I gotta ask you something, Mickey" were the first words out of Paul's mouth when he walked into our kitchen. Paul ambled over to the first cupboard to the right of the sink, grabbed a cup, and poured himself a steaming cup 'o mud from the ever-working coffee pot. He slid his lean frame on what we called the cleaner bench against the long wall of the farmhouse's kitchen. (That bench earned the name by being long, the inside divided into two sections for the vacuum cleaner to be stored, and still be sturdy seating for at least five little fannies.)

"Okay, what's up?" My mother could see the perplexed look on Paul's face and knew this was going to be one of "those" conversations. Yes, the ones she relished because she knew anyone could talk to her about anything.

"I realize you guys have only been up here a couple of years, but have you heard about the haunted cemetery in Brasher?" Paul's eyebrows raised a notch as he stirred two spoonfuls of sugar into his cup. "I mean, it's getting around how you're into the spooky stuff and all that . . ." He wasn't being insulting, just honest. Mickey didn't mind people knowing about her interest in the afterlife, ESP, or anything that can't be explained from a textbook.

"I haven't been told a thing about any haunted cemetery around here, Paul. Then again, most people do get spooked about cemeteries, but I never understood that. Really, shouldn't they be relaxing? I mean, our final resting place and all that?"

I grinned as I remembered going on picnics in cemeteries when we were all younger. We didn't have any money to go to the movies or amusement parks, so Ma would make some sandwiches and cookies, fill a couple of jars with Kool-Aid, and we'd head to a cemetery to explore then have lunch. Looking back on it now, I can see where those trips were definitely educational. We learned math: How old was Mr. Jones when he died? Subtract his birth year from his death year. How long were the Smiths married? What was the age difference between the children and their parents? Yes, plenty of math to do at a cemetery. Bible verses were abundant, especially on the older stones. Some were just chapter and verse, so we'd have to look them up in the Bible if we remembered to bring one that day, or we'd write the chapter/verse down and check it out when we went home. It wasn't about pounding religion into our heads; it was about learning. We learned what was important to those people on whose graves we carefully trod. Our eyes were opened to what values those departed souls held dearly in their mortal lives. Most were concerned with meeting the Lord. Others had a sense of humor and were, dare I say, even playful. I've seen headstones with images of deer chiseled on them. Either the person lying under that stone loved to hunt, or he loved nature's beasts. Maybe a bit of both. On many older stones I've noticed hands in prayer, or an open Bible etched into the granite. Every monument tells a story, whether it's an obvious one or maybe a puzzle for those left to solve.

Back to Paul's question. No, my mother hadn't heard about this particular cemetery. "It's the Fairview Cemetery right in Brasher. Just go straight past Lil's and take a right like you're going to Brasher Center. It's on the edge of town on the right-hand side. It's not very big, but it's the most haunted cemetery around here." Paul's eyes were big as he started describing what many people had told him. "Personally, I've never walked around in there. I've been by it hundreds of times but never had to go to a burial in that cemetery." My mother nodded and asked him to go on with specifics.

Many times these "hauntings" can be explained rationally. Is there a small brook or river nearby? Well then, there's your "mysterious" fog at night. Just moisture in the air when the temperature gets low enough to create a mist. Odd noises? Well, sure. There's no solid wall around the area, so you're going to get raccoons, chipmunks, skunks, squirrels, and any other varmints digging around in there. People leave special "treats" for their loved ones. Sometimes you'll see candy bars, hard candies, Twinkies, and even "puke peanuts" placed on stones. The mourners know their loved ones aren't going to reach up from the grave and grab the snacks, but it's a comforting gesture to show our dearly departed we're still thinking of them. The critters surely appreciate our little gifts, don't they? As far as sounds go, c'mon. You're in a place full of monuments of varying heights, widths, and weights. Anyone who can whistle knows what happens when a little bit of air travels through an area that has obstructions.

"I'm telling you, Mickey, that place is haunted. From what I've heard, you can actually SEE certain people by some of their stones. And sometimes the grass is flattened in a body shape." Paul's voice went up an octave and he started jabbering faster. "Sometimes smoke swirls around this one guy's stone. They say you can SMELL it. It's not fog."

"Would you happen to know which graves or spirits are the most active? Is there any particular time of day or night when people have experienced these events? Do you know of anyone else who will tell me about this particular cemetery?" Mickey liked to do her research and wanted more to go on than just a spooked neighbor.

"I don't think many people will talk about it. You know, nobody wants to be seen as crazy," Paul explained. "No offense meant!" he quickly added.

"None taken," my mother assured him with a grin.

The conversation went on like this for a little while longer, and Paul said he'd do some homework and come back soon. Sure enough, within a week, he returned. As he walked into the kitchen, he skipped the coffee pot and walked straight to my mother at the far end of the big kitchen table. He reached into his back pocket and pulled out a folded piece of notebook paper. Paul handed it to Mickey and said, "Here! Here's the names that I could get. They're the ones that are, as you say, active."

Mickey unfolded the paper and found seven names scribbled. "So, are these the graves, or the people who have experienced some weird stuff at this cemetery?"

"Oh, those are the dead people! Those are the ones who are haunting the cemetery the most. I'll bet there are more, but the old timers I talked to gave me these names. Some of the geezers gave me one or two names, but a few of them were repeated, so I KNOW that place is haunted. Will you go check it out sometime?" Paul's face reminded Mickey of a little kid who was double dog daring his friend to do something either stupid or scary.

"Hell yes, I'll check it out," was my mother's quick reply. "You'll want to come with me, right?"

"NO WAY!" Wow. That was fast. Paul didn't even bother to think about it.

Mickey laughed and said, "That's okay. I didn't think you'd want to go, but I had to offer. I always taught my kids to offer, even if you know the answer. Whether it's a helping of spaghetti or going to a haunted cemetery." Her mischievous grin brought a snicker from Paul.

"I'd rather have your spaghetti."

That following Monday my mother asked me if I wanted to go on an errand in Brasher. Usually my father went to Agway, the bank, or the hardware store, so I knew something was up right away. Without questioning her, I smiled and slipped my sneakers on my feet and followed her out the door. It was late afternoon and not anywhere near dark. We climbed into our 30-foot Ford LTD station wagon and pointed it toward Brasher. "Are you going to tell me what we're doing or where we're going?" I asked. With a grin and a sideways glance, my mother just gave me a nod.

"Supposedly there's a little activity in the cemetery outside of Brasher. We're just going to take a peek."

We drove through the tiny hamlet of Brasher Falls. Lil's bar was on our left, Bill's barbershop on our right. We went straight, with the old octagon house standing proudly on the left side of the street. Ma turned the car to the right and slowly inched our land yacht out of town. Sure enough, there was Fairview cemetery at the edge of the village. Ma swung the car wide to get it into the narrow gateway. She pulled in and drove to the back part of the graveyard and put the car in park. She shut it off and looked at me.

"Rumor has it there's something going on here. Let's find out!" And with a conspiratory look on her face, she handed me a piece of paper and a pen. "If you feel anything, write down where you are or the name on the stone where you feel it." I nodded and noticed she had a pen and paper in her hand too. She exited the Ford and I followed. "Just walk around and see if you get anything."

Mickey walked toward the left side of the cemetery, and I started wandering toward the right. We were the only people there and it was a quiet afternoon. No wind, it wasn't raining, and nobody was being planted that day. We had the place all to ourselves. Or so I thought. As I wandered among the stones, now and then I felt the urge to reach out and place my hand on certain ones. Sometimes I'd get a warm feeling. Other times I'd feel cold, almost sad. I glanced over and saw my mother doing the same thing. Her hands hovered over certain stones. She'd pause at a particular grave, then slowly move along to the next row of headstones. We both made notes.

We slowly stepped among the graves showing respect and reverence for the mortal remains beneath our feet and for the souls who may still be lingering. Now and then I felt a pocket of warm air that seemed to envelop my body, but only for a moment. Further along, there was a heaviness in my chest. There were odd smells that weren't exactly food smells, yet not unpleasant, perhaps reminiscent of perfume, but only a faint whiff. There weren't any flowering trees or bushes around and no freshly laid bouquets. Occasionally, I thought I saw a shadow or two wrapping around certain headstones. I made notes of all of these things and finally met up with my mother back at the car.

"Well?" That's it. Just a one-word question from her.

"You first," was my reply.

She held her paper out in front of her and read off a list of names. Mickey then went on to describe the shadows she saw leaning against two of the gravestones. She smelled a subtle rose perfume. In one area she smelled pipe tobacco. Her feet felt super cold on one grave in particular, so she moved off that one fast. Mickey described walking through warm pockets near this grave and that one. As she went through her list, I glanced down at mine. I had three of the same people listed on my paper. Then it was my turn. I did the same thing she did. I gave her my rendition of what I experienced in the previous hour or so that we'd been walking around that cemetery. I told her I never once felt freaked out or scared, just aware we weren't alone.

Then she pulled out her list from Paul. When we compared the names, between the two of us, we had collected all seven names on his list and more. Mickey had purposely kept his list to herself. She didn't want to influence me or give me a cheat sheet. Not that it would have mattered. What we both felt that day was real. The old-timers were not lying. The locals were not making up stories to tell on Halloween. There is definitely plenty of activity in the Fairview Cemetery in Brasher Falls, New York.

We went home that afternoon and Ma called Paul. He came over immediately and wanted to hear all about our findings. After relaying every tiny detail of our visit to Fairview, Paul smacked the table with his open palm and said, "I KNEW IT! I KNEW IT!" and started laughing. Mickey offered to take him over there sometime and show him the most active areas, but Paul again quickly declined.

"But nothing can hurt you, Paul."

"Doesn't matter. Cemeteries give me the creeps. All that

'activity' as you call it can stay there." Paul was dead serious. (Pun intended.)

Now and then when we had the time or if we were going in that direction anyway, my mother and I would pop into the Fairview and walk around. I remember one particular day she had a small bag of butter mints in her hand. As we walked around, she opened the bag and offered me some. I grabbed a couple and delighted in the quick melting confection on my tongue. She said, "I call these old people mints. If you go into old people's homes, they always seem to have these mints in a candy dish on their coffee tables." Mickey then reached into the bag and pulled a couple of candies and carefully placed them on a stone. She repeated this offering nine more times. A calm, warm feeling caressed the cemetery that afternoon. My mother reiterated the same sentiment every time: Nobody likes to be forgotten. It's always nice to let them know they're remembered.

With loving kindness, gratitude, and respect, our thanks go out to:

Florence Hall Latrace
Harry L. Mason
Dr. George F. Hall
Louis E. Bell
Margaret Carter
John Stevens and his two wives
Hiram E. Nash
And the several white stones that couldn't be read. We saw you.

MAGIC MUSIC

"'Cause I've been a wild catter, and a go-go getter, been an S.O.B. right down to the letter . . ." he sang softly as he wiped off the table next to me. This employee was dressed in dark blue Dickies pants and a light blue shirt that were ironed perfectly. His sandy blond hair was cut short and appeared to be a bit curly. I imagine if it was any longer, he'd have ringlets. I looked at his face and it was filled with joy. He had a portable CD player attached to his hip with a cord reaching up to the earphones firmly planted on his ears. I could tell the young man cleaning the tables at the mall had Down Syndrome but that obviously didn't stop him from doing his job and enjoying it. He looked at the table he had just wiped down and smiled with the satisfaction of a job well done. Perfectly smooth. Not a crumb or drop of soda left on it. He looked over at my table, checking to see if I was leaving or not. I could tell he was waiting to move on to his next mission. I looked up at him, smiled, and sang lightly, "I've had misadventures, I've even got pictures, I'm even more than I can stand . . ."

His left hand slid down his side fast and he clicked his CD player off. He reached up with his other hand, still holding the wiping rag, and pulled his earphones down around his neck.

"You know that song?" he asked excitedly.

"I sure do! That's Gary Allan! That's off his first CD, isn't it?" I replied.

""Her Man." That's the name of the song. Yeah, it's a really good record. Well, I guess it's not really a record. Those are played on record players with turntables and a little needle that makes the music go to the speakers." His smile was ear to ear. He'd found someone with the same taste in music and was happy to talk about it.

It wasn't very busy in the Salmon Run Mall that day in 1997. I was eating a late lunch, so the busy crowd had already dispersed. I'd gone to Watertown to return my then-boyfriend's two kids to their mother. The weekend was over, so they had to go back to their mom. It's about a two-hour drive each way, so I thought I'd walk around the mall for half an hour or so, grab a bite to eat, then head back to Massena. Even then I didn't like sitting in a car for hours at a time.

"I'm Pendra," I said as I offered my hand.

"I'm Richard, but everyone calls me Richie," was his response.

"Pleased to meet you, Richie. How long have you worked here?"

"Umm . . . I've been here for two Christmases. They always hire extras for the holidays. I got to stay because they like how I clean the tables and sweep up the floor."

He was an excellent worker. I could tell just from watching him for a few minutes. He wiped other tables as we chatted. He swept around those tables and emptied the dustpan into a bin on his cart. He definitely put my housekeeping skills to shame and for a fleeting moment I thought about kidnapping him, but rational thoughts got the better of me. I don't look good in prison orange.

"Do you listen to magic music?" Richie's head cocked to one side as he asked me this question.

"I'm not really sure what you mean by magic music. I listen to all sorts of music. Well, except rap. But I listen to most everything else. What's magic music?"

That's when he beamed me a huge smile. His eyes lit up like he'd just seen his first Christmas tree. "Hold on! I'll show you!" He dashed over to his janitor cart and pulled out a small CD wallet. It looked like it might have held 10-15 CDs. He came back over to my table, sat down, and unzipped his CD carrier.

"This," he said proudly, "is magic music!" He let me thumb through his collection. It was a mix of Gary Allan, Nat King Cole, Frank Sinatra, Johnny Cash, Bob Seger and a few more. Quite a collection, especially for someone as young as Richie, whom I placed in his mid-20s. "The music's in here," he said as he tapped the CDs, "but the magic's in here," as he patted his heart.

"Those are some really great singers, but what makes them magic? I was really curious as to what makes a certain artist magic. Or was it the music he was referring to when he claimed the magic existed? That's when he looked at me and rolled his big brown eyes. He was trying to be patient with me, but, you know, I could tell he was loving it. He was getting to explain how magic music worked.

"Here!" he exclaimed as he pulled his headphones off and placed them on me. "Now hold on . . ." As he thumbed through his collection, I watched the intent look on his face. Obviously, he was trying to figure out which cd was the most magical. He stopped about halfway through his collection, looked me in the eye, but didn't say a word. Something passed between us at that moment. It was a strange connection that I couldn't put my finger on. The CD he had pulled part of the way out of the sleeve was then pushed back. His fingertips walked further through the pocketed flaps until he came to the one he wanted and pulled it out. "This one. This one is magic for you." And with a smooth movement, he reached down, popped open the lid of the player, and changed out Gary Allan for whatever one he'd just selected. "Now just look up at the windows and listen." Richie pointed up to the ceiling where the windows let the bright light shine down upon us. I did as I was told. I knew this young man was on to something and I was anxious to see what it was. He looked down at his player on his hip and he hit the "forward" button several times until he came to the song he wanted. I waited. Then Bob Seger's voice started singing, "Seems like yesterday, but it was long ago . . ."

I had to catch my breath. I sat there stunned. Richie sat there smiling. I was still looking upward at the bright light coming through the windows and all at once the tears started welling up in my eyes then they spilled over to my cheeks. I lowered my face and just stared at this young man. I was silently crying, yet smiling, and listening to "Against the Wind." Richie was nodding at me. When the song was over, I pulled the earphones off my head and placed them on the table between us. He clicked the off button on his hip. "See? Magic." He lightly touched his palm to his chest, right over his heart.

Back in 1985 my brother Tyler was killed by a drunk driver. His favorite musical artist was Bob Seger and every time I hear one of Bob's songs, I think of my brother and how much I miss him. His senseless, tragic death at only 26 years old left a huge hole in my heart. Since Tyler's death, Bob Seger's songs have comforted me and made me smile. Even with tears in my eyes, they've made me smile. Once in a while I'll get in my car and say, "Hey Tyler! If you're around, gimme a sign!" Then I'll flip on the radio and a Bob Seger song will start to play. I know it's just a happy coincidence, but it makes me feel good. Makes me feel like I still have that connection with my brother.

I wiped my eyes with my napkin and started laughing. "How did you know?" I asked him. I'd never met this guy before. He didn't know my family. What kind of knowledge did this guy possess? "That was my brother's favorite singer. He's not here anymore, so I always think of him when I hear Bob Seger." I wanted to make sure Richie knew I wasn't crying because he upset me or made me sad.

"I just knew," was all he said as he shrugged his shoulders. Richie's big brown eyes held mine and for a brief moment I could have sworn I saw Tyler looking back at me. I know it was just my imagination. I know it was just wishful thinking influenced by hearing Bob Seger singing "Against the Wind."

I slid his earphones across the table and thanked him for letting me hear his magic music. "Not all music is magic," he told me. "Only certain songs are magic. Only the ones that you can feel inside your heart."

I nodded and told him I totally got it, that I understood

perfectly.

Richie stood up. "I'd better get back to work now. They count on me to have this area clean, so I'd better go." He then slipped his headphones back on, tapped the "play" button, and smiled down at me. He gave a wave good-bye. I smiled and waved back and watched him carry on with his cleaning.

My two-hour ride back to Massena didn't seem so long that afternoon. I'd like to tell you I flipped on the radio and heard a Bob Seger song, but that didn't happen. No sense in getting greedy.

GLASS CASTLES

Jealousy. I can pretty well sum up my relationship with jealousy and envy easily enough. I'm guessing it's a lot like yours. We might have a few differences, but I think we're all basically the same.

Was it instilled in us from birth? I don't believe we picked it up from others because we're inherently jealous even as tiny children. You see another niblet of a human being playing with a toy and BAM! I WANT THAT! You may have several perfectly good toys to amuse you in your lap, but you want whatever is in that other child's sticky little hands. At that age it's all visual. We see something. We want it. Plain and simple.

Later on, we get jealous of parental attention, especially if one has siblings. How dare my mother pay attention to my older brother? Just because he fell down, scraped his knee, and a river of blood is flowing to his ankle, does that merit all this special attention from her? Now the resentment starts forming, jealous over the attention he's sopping up and resenting the hell out of him for taking our mother's focus off ME. The other siblings made their moves too. A cut here, a bellyache there. It was hell to have to share my parents' attention with those five other selfish roommates.

Moving right along, we head to school where we mingle with other imps our own age. We still haven't advanced from that selfish stage where every toy is MINE, but we're put in our place and reminded to share. Share? With total strangers? Dang. Bad enough I have to share with all my siblings at home, but now you want me to give up my rights in this big building crammed with non-family members? I don't know how long I'll be able to handle this place and these rules. Turns out it gets better with time. Either that or we just get used to it.

The middle school years are soon upon us and that's when things start to get a little testy. Unless we're rich enough and privileged enough to go to a parochial school where uniforms make everyone equal, we're now faced with fashion jealousy. Being a poor farm kid with no-name denim jeans, plain t-shirts, and Ames sneakers, it wasn't too hard to become jealous of the rich kids in school. They had all the latest in fashion from the cool hip hugger bell bottom pants to the luxurious sweater vests. And there I was, with my plain pocket jeans and my best t-shirt that had a cartoon kitten over where my breasts would eventually develop. I sulked through that stage, quietly hoping nobody would notice my blandness.

Things became even tougher in high school. Hormones raging, wanting to be pretty, hoping to be noticed, but still only blending in with the shadows of the open locker doors. Sneaking looks at the jocks, knowing they'd never look back. Still, sighing as they walked by was a guilty pleasure. Popular girls wore short skirts and pantyhose. On the rare days I wore a dress, down to my knees, I was still in knee socks. Nerd doesn't even begin to come close to describing my fashion sense. I didn't have braces or glasses, so I had that going for me, right? Ahh, the jealousy I felt watching those girls who had it all together. They were cute, perky, popular, and never even had to try to look good. They just did.

All that envy as a youngster trains us for the pangs we feel as adults. We see someone with a better car and we covet that. The guy down the street just put up a new three-car garage. The boss just took a trip to Hawaii and the furthest I've been is to Syracuse. Ugh. It's never enough and we always want more. We're taught to be happy for those who work and earn nice possessions or vacations. For the most part, we ARE happy for those people, but that jealousy still simmers deep down in our guts. We're human. We're going to want what others have.

The best part about getting older is you realize what a waste of time jealousy can be. Oh sure, it serves a purpose when you're young. It makes you want to work harder to earn more money to buy all those desired items or trips. You work double shifts, shorten your vacations, and take a second job. You put your body through hell to get that almighty dollar so all your dreams can come true. Then, one day, if you've worked hard enough and if the Fates are smiling down upon you, you get there. You have that nice home and car. You're dressed in snazzy clothing and jewelry. You take trips to parts of the world you've only seen in magazines or on television. You've made it.

That sweet sigh of relief and the pleasure of victory is yours. Taking a look around, you see others who are just like you. They've worked their butts off and have made a decent life for themselves too. These are your people. You're happy for them. No more envy. No more jealousy. Just a smile and a silent nod in their direction because you know they're sitting pretty the way you are.

Or are they?

I was recently having a discussion with my close friend Ruthie Sanford about people who seem to have it all yet are still jealous of others. They have great homes, vehicles, retirement plans, and their health. They brag about their flawless family members who never make mistakes. Everything in their lives is rosy and nothing but sunshine. And yet, they feel it's necessary to tear others down who weren't as fortunate to have had excellent paying jobs. Or maybe their homes aren't picture perfect. It's a sport for them to knock down anyone else's dreams if they differ from their own. Heaven forbid someone else accomplishes something they themselves never dared to try. Ruthie said these people live in glass castles. I think she nailed it. They want the world to think their lives are perfect. They project this superior attitude and want everyone to believe their lives are worth envying. Maybe it's because I came from genuinely modest beginnings that I can appreciate all walks of life. I admit, I cringe when I drive by a house that has those big, ugly plastic toys sitting in the weedy front yard. I'm not a fan of rusting cars jacked up on blocks. Using old tarps for curtains isn't my thing. But guess what? If that's the best they can do, or if they're happy with it, leave them alone. The people behind that closed front door are probably less stressed and a lot happier than most people living in their million-dollar glass castles.

When I see someone succeed at their job, hobby, or personal goal, I'm genuinely happy for them. I'll give credit where it's due and cheer louder than anyone else. It takes absolutely nothing from me to build someone else up, so I try to do that every chance I get. I appreciate it so much when someone helps me achieve my goals or dreams. Sometimes it's just hearing "Hey, go for it!" or "I'm proud of you!" I don't need a parade, but knowing people are sincerely happy for me and can acknowledge achievements I accomplish means the world to me.

I will never understand these glass castle people. We all know someone like this. We also know what's going on in the background. Their lives are NOT perfect. They have family estrangements. They have skeletons hidden in their closets. They have false friendships because they want to be seen with the "right" people. They join certain clubs or organizations because they relish that pompous feeling they get. They put on airs because we're supposed to be impressed with whatever they're doing but, honestly, we don't care. Still, they're living such shallow lives that image is everything. They think they're fooling the world when they're only fooling themselves. But are they? Really? I don't point this out because of jealousy. I wouldn't want that kind of life where image is everything. I prefer to be REAL. I admit I'm a low-maintenance woman. I'm as real as you'll ever get. No phony stuff for me. I do believe you can have beautiful things and a great life, but don't go out of your way to project perfection because nobody's life is perfect. And actually, it's insulting if you think we all believe your fairytale.

I have to feel sorry for these people in a way. They've "made it" and are super successful in the material sense. Unfortunately, they're bankrupt in the real happiness department. Being under the pressure to constantly project that false perfect image must be exhausting. Never knowing when someone will find out about your imperfect life or situation must be stressful. I'm sure it takes a lot of energy to keep that glass castle shining and looking impeccable all the time.

As for me, I'll stick to my modest little house with the pretty flowers out front. I know my home is a place where everyone feels comfortable, and nobody envies anything I have. The people who visit me have good hearts and they know I've worked for all I have, as simple as it is. Some of my friends have much nicer homes. Some have homes that are not as fancy. But guess what? I don't care. And neither do they. We're in this for friendship, not for material wealth or a false image. I'll take someone who is real over a phony any day of the week. I prefer to wrap myself in the warmth of honest, sincere friends than to put on a false face and pretend to be something and someone I'm not.

We've all seen them, these people in their glass castles. And in the end, they're left alone and lonely because their lies and deceptions will always be made known and that's when the glass will start to crack and everything in their pretend world will come crashing down on them in tiny cutting splinters and shards.

OSCAR'S CANE

Way back in the late 1980's, my older brother had to go to Texas for a week or so. His job sent him there to pick up a few new skills that he could use for their company in Kentucky. While my brother was there, he had a little bit of down time in the evenings, so he wandered around the local shops. He wasn't much of a shopper, but this one particular item caught his eye, and he just knew he had to purchase it for Oscar. A few weeks went by and a package from Kentucky arrived at Rural Route #1, Brasher Falls, New York. Oscar carefully opened the box and inside was the most beautiful cane he'd ever seen. The paperwork explaining what the cane was made of, and who made it was enclosed. Oscar was delighted to say the least.

That special cane accompanied Oscar everywhere for the following months. If he went to Agway, he carried it with him. To the bank in Winthrop? Absolutely. Up to North Lawrence for the Sunday paper? Why not?

One day Oscar was headed into North Lawrence to restock his supply of cigars. He never wore a watch, but he could time anything with his cigars. How long does it take to plow that end field? Two and a half cigars. How much time did he spend fixing the corn picker? Only one cigar. Oscar's cigars were his trademark and now he had this special cane to add to his persona. On that particular day in NoLaw (as the locals call it), Oscar saw two ladies he knew heading into the town's restaurant. I'm going to call these two ladies Mrs. Smith and Mrs. Jones out of respect and maybe even out of apologies for what happened that day.

Oscar parked his pickup truck at the store and walked over to the restaurant. When he entered, he noticed the two ladies he had seen walking in moments before were seated with two other women. These women were all in their 40's or 50's, around Oscar's age. Oscar mosied up to their table and said good morning to all of the women. Pleasantries were exchanged for a bit and finally one of them noticed Oscar's cane and asked him about it. Oscar looked down, almost as an afterthought, and said, "Oh, yes, my son just gave this to me a little while ago and I really enjoy it. Isn't it beautiful?" He raised his cane chest level and turned to his right and left so everyone in the diner could see it. The restaurant was so small that every person could hear their conversation, and naturally the rest of the people were interested in Oscar's new cane. The ladies all agreed it was a fine-looking cane.

"Here. Hold it and see how light yet sturdy it is," he said as he handed his accessory to Mrs. Smith. She held it in her hands, balanced it in the middle, and commented on how lovely the twist in it was. Then she passed it to Mrs. Jones. Oscar spoke up and told her to run her hand along the whole thing, from the handle all the way down to the little rubber knob at the bottom. Did she feel any burrs? Nope! Just that smooth, solid, blond wood. Then Oscar said, "If you warm the wood up with your hand, you can even smell a faint scent it carries." No way! So, Mrs. Jones proceeded to rub the cane vigorously then lifted it under her nose to take a whiff. "Can you smell that faint aroma?" he asked.

"I think I can. I'm not really sure. Let me warm it up again." And she did. She rubbed the wooden cane harder then quickly placed it under her nose to take a sniff. "Yes! I can smell it now!" she exclaimed with a smile.

"You can even taste the sweetness of it if you put the tip of your tongue on it!" Oscar chimed in excitedly.

"Really?" Mrs. Jones rubbed it with fervor again then quickly touched the tip of her tongue to the cane where she had warmed it with the friction of her hands. "I think I DO taste something. It's sort of sweet. Is that just the varnish on it, or is it the wood itself? What kind of wood IS this, Oscar?"

Ahh, the moment he'd been waiting for had arrived. The fish had taken the bait. That's when Oscar figured he'd done enough damage. "It's a bull's dick, straight from Texas!" He made sure he said it loud enough for all the patrons in the restaurant to hear.

Mrs. Jones threw the cane at Oscar and called him several words that had probably never before escaped her lips in her lifetime. She reached for her napkin and was wiping her tongue in disgust. Mrs. Smith had a few choice words and comments to peg him with too. What they suggested he could do with that cane would have made a sailor blush.

The rest of the diners were in stitches. One of them hollered over, "YOU SHOULD HAVE KNOWN BETTER! THAT'S OSCAR!" And it's true. These ladies should have known better. They knew what kind of man Oscar was and that he'd take advantage of anyone - in a kind way - for a laugh.

It took a while for the ladies to forgive him, but they never forgot.

Before my father died, he gave that cane to my cousin for safekeeping. He said it was too special to be buried with him, so now my cousin Dave has a sentimental memento from Uncle Oscar. Where it'll end up, we don't know. All I know is Oscar sure did get a lot of mileage from that special cane from Texas.

STONE-COLD SOBER

Ninety-two degrees with high humidity. That's how hot it was in late July. I've never been a fan of cruel weather. I consider it cruel when the thermometer goes above eighty or below zero. So really, there's plenty of happy space on my thermometer. But ninety-two? C'mon! That's just not necessary at all. I wasn't in the sidewalk egg frying business. This picnic I'd been invited to, no . . . wait. Not invited to, but guilt tripped into, was going to be crowded. No pool, just sprinklers for the kids. I thought about taking a plastic lawn chair and placing it where the hose could spit at me every twelve seconds. Nope. I'm an adult now so all the other grown-ups would be expecting me to join them at the picnic tables. I begged whatever gods may be that the hosts had at least set up some tents or canopies. They said they'd have everything and to bring nothing. Well, guess again. I was taught you NEVER show up empty handed. I tossed the last of the ice from my freezer into the cooler holding two 12-packs of Labatt Blue Light and six bottles of water. I closed the cooler's lid and hoisted it. Not too heavy. It would certainly count as not going empty handed. My mother would have been proud.

I took my time driving over to the D'Angelo homestead. The a/c in my car was blasting on high but it barely made a dent in the day's violations of my right to be comfortable. I sulked. I already had a heat headache. I was getting pre-cranky before I even entered the party. How did I let my friends guilt trip me into attending this get-together? Oh yeah, I remember. I had done something nice for their kid who had just finished his first year of college. They wanted to say thank you, so they invited me to come stuff my belly and drink as much as I could hold. No good deed goes unpunished, right?

The D'Angleos had a nice older home out in the country. It really wasn't too far from town, but it felt like it was in the boonies. When I arrived, there had to have been at least twenty cars parked along the winding driveway and onto the well-manicured lawn. I pulled into a spot that wouldn't block anyone and killed the engine. Within 2.2 seconds I felt like a Thanksgiving turkey in an unyielding oven. I quickly glanced down at my left boob for a popped-up tab, but there wasn't one. I wasn't done yet. Damn. I opened my door, and a tidal wave of oppressing heat slapped me like I had insulted Mother Nature and for some reason deserved her backhand. I reached into my back seat for the cooler of Blues and headed toward the back yard. Sweat was already trickling between my shoulder blades. My hair hung limply like overcooked spaghetti. I had a dewy mustache, and my forehead was glistening. (Side note: My mother always told me horses sweat, men perspire, and ladies glisten.) I was glistening like a pig.

I rounded the corner of the house and saw the tents and tarps held up by sturdy poles. The ropes anchoring them were adorned with pool noodles so people would see them and not catch a shin and go flying ass over teakettle. Way off to one side the sprinklers and hoses were set up. They even had a slip-n-slide which I figured I could probably do right now sans garden hose. I was met by the lady of the house, Frannie. "Oh! You didn't have to bring anything! You're our guest! Come over and fill a plate. Plenty of food and tons of coolers. Please, dig in!"

I was drenched but so was everyone else. "We're all in this together" seemed to be the motto of that melting pot. I grabbed a plate and loaded a few bites of food on it. I don't know about you, but when it's painfully hot I don't get very hungry. With my sustenance in one hand and my cooler in the other, I meandered over to the biggest tent because I noticed there were several standing fans in there. Yes, please! I found a comfy chair, kicked back in the direct line of the fan's life-giving breath, and nibbled from my plate. Several other guests had the same idea and we all exchanged pleasantries with smiles and waves. I knew most of the family and quite a few of the other guests, so conversation flowed easily. After I tossed my empty paper plate into the trash, I returned to my seat and popped open my cooler. I grabbed a cold beer and offered beers to all of my companions who were also enduring this sweltering day. A few grabbed my chilled offerings, but when I turned to my right and proffered a Labatt to my acquaintance, he said no thanks. Okay, I thought, sometimes people don't like beer when it's too hot. Maybe this guy gets dehydrated easily. Or maybe he's in AA. Either way, I know enough to not push it when someone refuses booze. It's their business and none of mine. I knew Jarred was a friend of the family but didn't really know him well. I'd only seen him a handful of times at social functions.

Conversations rolled on and people came and went from our little congregation in front of the big fans. Eventually, I was left alone with my non-drinking friend. We had a lot in common, both of us having grown up on small dairy farms, so we laughed about life as country bumpkins and look at us now. Then he asked me something, "Hey, aren't you the one who likes all that spooky stuff? You know, like crazy things that happen to people that can't be explained?"

I smirked a little bit wondering how those conversations come up with other people. Oh yeah, talk to her, she's a space cadet! "Yeah, I like crazy stories. I like things that give me goosebumps or freak me out a little bit. Why? Do you have a good one?"

"I do. I've told only a few people about it, but I get laughed at a lot. And, man, I totally get it. I understand because it's really out there, you know?" He shrugged his shoulders and rolled his eyes up toward his brain.

"Well, now you gotta tell me!" I said as I reached into my cooler for a second beer. I left the cooler lid open and tipped it toward my chat buddy letting him see there was beer and water, and he could help himself. He looked in, gave a smile, and grabbed a bottle of water.

"Thanks for the water. That beer looks great, but I stopped drinking in 1992. As a matter of fact, I can tell you it was at 8:32 p.m. on March 4th, 1992." He stated with such precision.

"Umm . . . that's pretty well narrowed down. Most people say the year, or maybe even the month they quit drinking. But you know the exact moment? If it bothers you if I drink, I can put my beer down. I don't need it." I made a motion to put my beer back in the cooler, but he waved his hand at me.

"No. No, that's okay. Other folks drinking doesn't bother me at all. I'm not one of THOSE people. Haha." Jarred's face was smiling sincerely. He appreciated the fact that I didn't want to offend him or entice him with my cold one.

He began, "You didn't know me when I was younger. I was a party dude in high school. I was one of the popular guys. I was an average student, did just enough to get by and not get kicked off the sports teams for scholastic slacking. I played hard, but I also partied hard. I loved going out with the guys after a game and getting hammered. After graduation I went into my dad's construction business for a little while and . . . well . . . construction workers like to tip a few too. I got into it pretty heavily. I was drinking too much and too often. One day at work I was really hungover, and I wrecked an expensive piece of equipment. My father was really angry with me and rightfully so. Nobody got hurt, but I screwed up his backhoe big time. That put the entire project behind and cost my dad a lot of money. He pulled me aside and told me I was done. In all honesty, he'd given me a few other chances before that, but I took it for granted that my dad would always cover for me and let me get away with it." Jarred's head lowered, and I could see shame and guilt hitting him hard. I remained silent and let him go on with his story.

"My folks had a talk and then made a few phone calls. They called my mother's brother, Uncle Chuck, and asked if he had any use for me. Now, I was totally against this because Uncle Chuck, also known as Charles, never Charlie, to non-family members, owned a funeral home. Good God. They wanted me to go work at a goddamned funeral home." Jarred's shoulders gave a shiver.

I stifled a laugh and said, "You couldn't pay me enough to work in a mortuary. Real-live dead people?" No thanks."

Jarred looked back at me and repeated my expression, "Real-live dead people. You're cute."

He shifted his weight in the lawn chair and took a slug of his cold water. "So, I ended up going to work for Uncle Chuck, but not because I wanted to. I went because I had blown every cent I had earned while working for my dad. I was still living at home, mooching off my folks, and telling them I was saving up for an apartment or house of my own soon. What really happened was I drank it all. I wasn't anywhere near moving out of the family home and my parents weren't really pushing me, so why should I make the effort? Yeah, I was a selfish kid." Hindsight is 20/20, isn't it? I could tell that's what was going through Jarred's mind.

"Jarred, I think we're all sort of selfish at that age. We don't have much responsibility, so we aren't aware of what's going on around us" I said, trying to give him an out, trying to ease his feelings of guilt.

"Well, it didn't matter. I showed up at UC's and he didn't pull any punches. I wasn't a licensed mortician, but I could do some of the grunt work. Not gonna lie, it friggin' creeped me out at first. Seeing old people naked is gross. I died a little bit inside anytime a little kid came in, whether they went from sickness or accidents. I'm telling you, you get a new view on life when you work with death every day. But I still drank. My uncle kept a good eye on me, and I had to show up sober every day. I was learning some of the ins and outs of death work, and at times it was almost interesting. I mean, as a young man it wasn't my life's goal to work with stiffs, but there is actually an art to it."

I nodded appreciatively and said, "I don't think I could ever do that job, but I'm sure glad others can. A lot like doctors and nurses. No way could I ever handle that stuff."

Jarred turned his chair slightly toward me. His face became serious as he looked around to make sure nobody else could overhear our conversation. "As I said, I was still young and still drinking. Uncle Chuck made sure I reported to work sober every day. He had me working mostly afternoons and evenings. Looking back at it now, I can figure out why he did that. Number one, it was because he was busy dealing with the families of the dead people during the day. He did most of the arrangements during morning hours. Number two, it finally clicked with me that if I drank at night, then maybe Uncle Chuck figured I'd have all morning to get sober and presentable. I didn't drink during the morning hours, so he knew I'd be okay to work in the afternoon and evening. If I worked with him until 8:00 or 9:00 at night, then I wouldn't be hammering down afternoon beers, right? He was pretty smart about condensing my drinking hours to a very short window." He smiled at this bit of logic on his uncle's part. He pulled himself forward in his chair. "Then that night happened." Jarred's face went a little bit white.

He had my full attention. He was getting to the good stuff, and I didn't want to miss a word.

"One Wednesday night I was working with UC down in the embalming room. He was at the first table getting 93-year-old Mrs. Donovan prepped for preservation, and I was washing down the second slab that was empty. You really do have to learn how to remove yourself mentally and emotionally when you're washing away hair, blood, and other body fluids that are pretty gross." My mind made a picture of this and I gagged slightly. "That's when the phone rang and I picked it up. It was Aunt Lena. I handed the phone to my uncle. Aunt Lena had just taken a tumble with the laundry basket down the cellar stairs and wanted Uncle Chuck to come home. She said she was a little bumped and bruised, but she might need to go to the emergency room. Uncle Chuck quickly hung up the phone and looked at me. He asked me to put Mrs. Donovan away and to finish cleaning up the shop, then lock up when I left. And away he ran."

"Was your aunt hurt badly? Did she have to go to the hospital?" I asked.

"No, she was fine. Just like she said, bumps and bruises, but she was a solid lady, and the laundry basket actually broke her fall. Thank God for dirty clothes, huh?" Jarred laughed at the thought of a basket of stinky clothes saving her life.

"I was alone down there in the embalming room. I'd gotten used to the dead bodies. I could handle the stink of the chemicals. No issues at all." Jarred's eyes widened slightly as he lowered his voice. "I will swear on a Bible that what happened next is the truth. I've gone over it in my head a million times, but I can't explain it rationally. I was wiping down the stainless-steel counter near the big sink. I thought I could hear something behind me, and it sounded like the trocar (the tube-like piece that sucks the juice out of people) that Uncle Chuck had been using on Mrs. Donovan. He had set it down next to her head when he left in a hurry to go help Aunt Lena. I turned around and it was sitting on Mrs. Donovan's stomach. I thought I must have imagined Uncle Chuck setting it down on the table near her head when he left and didn't think anything more of it. I turned and went back to wiping down the counter and sink. Then I heard another noise behind me and when I looked over my shoulder, the trocar was on the table next to Mrs. Donovan's head. My first thought was, okay, maybe Uncle Chuck had a spare sitting there all along and had left one on Mrs. Donovan's stomach too. But that was so unlike him. He only used one when he was working. I glanced at Mrs. Donovan's stomach, and it was bare. No implements on her belly. That's when I walked over and picked up the trocar that was near her head. I looked all over the table and around her body for the second one but didn't find it. There weren't any other tools on the table with Mrs. Donovan. By then I was laughing at myself. I was obviously making stuff up in my head, getting myself psyched up over being alone down there without Uncle Chuck. I tried to laugh it off as I grabbed a sheet and covered her up, getting her ready to put back in the crisper."

I looked at him, shock on my face. "Crisper?" I asked.

"Oh, sorry. That's what I called it. You know, like when you put stuff in the crisper in the fridge to keep fresh longer. I know it's disrespectful but, remember, I was just an immature kid doing a job I was forced to do. I guess I was still bitter and angry with my folks for making me work with Uncle Chuck," Jarred explained.

In my own twisted mind, I could see where he'd come up with that wording.

"So anyway, I took the trocar to the sink and started washing it too. Then I heard what I thought was a whisper, almost a whooshing noise. I turned the water off and waited. I was mentally talking to myself saying, 'knock it off, idiot!' When I turned back to the table, the sheet was off Mrs. Donovan's head. I know damned well I had pulled the sheet up over her head. Uncle Chuck had these special sheets just for covering the bodies. They're extra long but not quite as wide as a regular sheet. They're a light cotton, almost like gauze, but they're washable. Anyway, I stood with my back against the sink and just stared. And I swear I saw her lips moving slightly and I HEARD her saying, 'Stop the drink. The drink will kill you.'"

I wanted to laugh because this was something straight out of a book, or a scary movie. I knew I'd been had, and that he was about to laugh at how gullible I was. He got me fair and square. I fell for his story hook, line, and sinker. I was just about to crack a smile and smack him on the arm when I looked at Jarred's face and saw he had a tear rolling down his cheek. I didn't say a word. This wasn't a joke after all.

"I looked at my watch. It was 8:32 p.m. I glanced around the room to see if any of my buddies had somehow gotten inside and were messing with me, but no. They wouldn't have gone in there anyway, so it wasn't someone playing a joke on me. I stared back at Mrs. Donovan lying there on the table. I didn't hear anything else from her. No more whispering or whooshing noises. That's when I looked down and realized I'd wet myself. Yeah, I did. I was so scared and in shock that I pissed myself right there as I was pushed back against the big sink."

The hair on my arms was sticking straight up even though it was over 90 degrees that day. I felt a chill run down my spine and gave an involuntary shudder. Jarred looked at me. "Eventually I did end up putting Mrs. Donovan back in the fridge and finished cleaning the table she'd been on. It wasn't easy, but I did it. I went home, showered, and put my clothes in the washer. The next afternoon I went to work. Aunt Lena was fine, according to Uncle Chuck. He and I went downstairs to continue working on Mrs. Donovan. As I helped him get her set up so he could finish what he'd started the night before, I casually asked him, in a joking manner of course, if he ever felt spooked with the dead bodies. Did he ever 'hear' anything that he couldn't explain?"

Jarred was composed and calm as he relayed the short and simple conversation he and his uncle had that afternoon. "Uncle Chuck looked me dead in the eye, pardon the pun, and said yes. Yes, the dead people talk to him all the time. He said sometimes you only 'feel' them talking to you, other times you can hear them with your ears. He said it takes a special person to hear the dead and if you're chosen, it's a gift."

Wow. "I'm not so sure many people would want that gift, Jarred," I said.

"Yeah, you're right. I figured I'd be safe to tell you about this. I know about you and your mom . . . " his voice had dropped to a whisper. Hmm . . . apparently he knew about my mother's love of all the unexplained phenomena out there. I smiled inside.

"Your uncle never told people about this? Wait, I get it. You can't really talk about this because they'll lock you up in the loony bin." I'm a quick study.

Jarred bounced his head up and down. "DING! DING! You win a prize! Uncle Chuck didn't talk about it with other people because he had a small business to run. That was the day I told him about Mrs. Donovan's words to me. He knew I was serious, and he treated me with respect. He knew I'd experienced something real. March 4, 1992 at 8:32 p.m. was the beginning of my sobriety. I had been heading in a really bad direction. I can't believe I'm saying this, but a dead person saved my life. Looking back on my life now, I'm certain I would have either died in a car wreck or maybe developed cirrhosis of the liver and suffered for years before dying way too young. When I tell people I'm stone cold sober, I really mean it."

"Maybe Mrs. Donovan was sent to be your guardian angel?" I queried.

"She must have been. I didn't really know her when she was alive. I knew who she was but didn't really know her on a personal level. She must have seen I would turn out just fine with a little help. You wanna hear something really silly?" he asked.

"Go for it. Nothing you say is going to shock me now," I replied.

"Well, as you know, I went back to my dad's construction business and eventually took over for him. Every now and then, when I have a really hard day or if I think I might want to reach for a bottle, I think of Mrs. Donovan. I've even been to her grave a few times to pay my respects. And you know . . . I feel something. I can't explain it, but it's almost like a calmness comes over me when I remember her."

I assured Jarred what he was feeling wasn't silly. I loved how he still paid his respects to her and still offered his thanks to her for saving his life. I believed every single word of his story. I knew enough about him to know he was a good guy. Apparently, he'd had a rough start, but he's living proof people can and do change, even if it's with a little help from the most unlikely sources.

PICTURE THIS

When I was in my 20's, 30's, and 40's, I did a bit of traveling. I hit far-off destinations like Hawaii, New Zealand, Australia, and Fiji. I crossed the Atlantic to venture to Italy, Germany, France, Austria, Belgium, Luxembourg, the Netherlands, Switzerland, and Denmark. I've been to the city of Vancouver way out on the west coast of Canada and have also hit several towns in the provinces of Ontario and Quebec. The warmth and sunshine of the Bahamas and Jamaica were lovely. My travels right here in the good ol' U.S. of A. have been generous, but not extensive. From Alaska to Florida, I've enjoyed every single trip. Through it all, I've taken more pictures than I'll ever count. I have memories at which I look back and smile or laugh right out loud. I used to love to travel and experience different cultures, foods, and people. The kaleidoscope of currencies, dialects, and customs mesmerized me from an early age. I always knew this world was huge, but when traveling, it really hammers it home just how tiny we are in this big picture called life.

A few days ago, I was looking for a particular picture of my brother. I opened one of my many boxes of photos and ended up going down memory lane. I hadn't packed a lunch for this trip, but I should have. I ended up sitting on the floor of my office (spare bedroom that holds no bed) and reliving some of the adventures I'd had in my youth. Each picture has a story. Each expression was captured as I was living in the moment. Priceless. Then something pinged in my head and that's when the gray matter started churning. In many of the pictures, there are strangers in the background. This can't be helped when visiting the Colosseum in Rome or the Leaning Tower of Pisa. I giggled as I pondered how many other people's photos I am in. It only stands to reason I'd be in the background of some other eager tourist's photos. How many candid shots of me stuffing my face with real pizza or authentic chocolates does someone have sitting in a shoe box back home? Do I show up hoisting that beer stein with both hands? Am I staring too intently at the statue of David?

As I smirked to myself at these thoughts, I took a closer look at a few of my own snapshots. There's one of the Trevi Fountain in Rome where I was smiling a huge smile. I wasn't doing the cheesy tourist grin for the camera. I had the Cheshire Cat toothy grin because just a few feet behind my friend with the camera was a young couple. The man had just dropped to one knee and proposed to his lady at that very second. Being the hopeless romantic that I am, it made my smile bigger than usual. Now I wonder how that couple is doing. Are they still married? Do they still travel? Are they grandparents by now? I remember silently wishing these strangers all the best in their future together as they walked away from the fountain. I had no idea where they were from or where they were headed. I just know they shared their special moment not only with me, but with everyone surrounding Trevi Fountain that day. Now I wonder if anyone has this couple in the background of their pictures. Chances are, they do.

I came across some pictures I had taken when I was at the Seven Sacred Pools on the Hana Highway on Maui, Hawaii. I was trying to get different angles and eventually stood next to a gentleman who I had accidentally included in one shot. He had a serious look on his face as he reached into his pocket and selected a shiny penny from his palm. He held it tightly in his fist and said, "I WISH I'D GET THAT JOB!" and cast his copper hope into the water. I reached into my purse and pulled out a penny. I elbowed him lightly, smiled, then drew my arm back then flung it forward and loudly said, "I WISH HE'D GET THAT JOB!" He looked at me and started laughing. I shrugged my shoulders and told him it can't hurt, right? I hadn't thought about that guy in ages, but I wonder if he ever did get that job.

Down in Fiji, we were bussed around on an island tour. One of the stops was in a tiny ramshackle village. The local ladies made little clay figurines to sell to tourists, and I felt somewhat guilty if I didn't offer a dollar or two for these crude trinkets. While my niece and I were perusing their wares, I also took pictures. The ladies were all sitting on their woven mats on the dirt floor of this big hut. I was taking a picture of one vendor's selection of tiny clay turtles. I didn't notice it until I came home and had my pictures printed that there was an older woman sitting quite still in the corner of the hut. Looking at that picture made me sad. The woman I had accidentally snapped was obviously unhealthy. Her eyes looked dazed, and her skin was rough. I don't recall any movement from her the whole time we were shopping there. Now I wonder if that woman was dying. How long did she make it after our visit? Did I buy from the right woman so she'd have money to take care of this other woman?

Up in Alaska I was taking pictures of a totem pole in Ketchikan. I took several snaps because every time I thought I had a clear picture, someone would walk right in front of the pole and ruin it for me. ARGH! Look around, people. Be aware of your surroundings. I finally did get a good shot, but it came after I had to wait for this one couple that was arguing to step aside. They're still in the picture, and they're what I remember most about that moment. I had to stifle a laugh because they thought they were being quiet, but they were doing what I call scream whispering. The gist of their conversation was this: She cheated on him. He forgave her. The cruise was to save their 25-year marriage but it wasn't going to work if she kept flirting with every goddamned server, busboy, and bartender on the ship. Now when I see that picture of the totem pole, I'm not thinking of Alaska as much as I am servers, busboys, and bartenders.

While heading out for a zip-line excursion in Jamaica, I accidentally took a picture of . . . umm . . . what I'll refer here to as a "spice deal" between a local vendor and a passenger from the cruise ship. I was taking a picture of the ship from a street that was angled up a little bit from the docking area. I took several pictures and again, not noticing anything until later. Right there on the left-hand side of the beautiful picture of our ship, is a guy handing another guy a wad of American bills and that second guy handing back a small bulging envelope. Probably just some tasty Jamaican oregano, right? Still, I laughed as I remembered being offered spices all day when we were on the island. I doubt there are any candid shots where a spice deal wasn't going down.

One of the saddest backgrounds I noticed was taken at a casino in Las Vegas. Guests are discouraged from taking pictures where the card tables are, but security doesn't mind so much at the slot machines. I had just sat down, fed a sawbuck into my machine, and pulled the lever on the one-armed bandit. Nothing happened. I pulled it again, and the bells and whistles started making noise. Not a lot, but enough. I didn't win huge. No million bucks, no car, no trip to Tahiti. But I did win $300 on that ten-dollar investment. One of the cocktail waitresses was going by at that moment and offered to take my picture with my big win. I smiled like the goober that I am. Later on, sitting in my room, I was scrolling through the pictures on my little digital camera. There I was, all country bumpkin happy over my lucky spin of $300. That's when I noticed behind me was a man slumped over, a look of total defeat on his face. I think he may have been crying. He was dressed poorly and looked like he needed sleep and a shower. I was totally oblivious to this man just a few seats beyond mine. Unfortunately, that sight is all too common in Las Vegas and any other casino-carrying town. My heart went out to this gentleman in my picture. The odds were against him. Casinos aren't in business to make you rich.

Now it's your turn. Think of all the places you've been and how many photos you're in accidentally. How many people have photo albums with your smiling face gracing a picture or two? Oh sure, you might be smiling off in another direction, but there you are. As I paw through my collection of memories on these little pieces of glossy paper, I'm reminded of how we're all connected in one way or another. These connections hold us, they keep us strong and make us feel like we belong. These strangers in my photos will never know I've thought of them and have wished them well. They'll never get a Christmas or birthday card from me. Does this matter? No. We can wish happiness and good luck on total strangers without shorting ourselves one bit. And who knows? Maybe, just maybe, there's a magic wish fairy out there who will hear us and make it happen for them. Wouldn't that be a hoot?

GETTING OLDER

I'm officially old. How do I know this? I've made a list.

1. For starters, every jacket I own has in its pockets at least one tube of Chapstick and several tissues. That's definitely an old lady starter pack.

2. I tend to eat my evening meal earlier now. I'm not a blue-plate maven just yet, but I'm beginning to understand why certain seniors prefer to eat at 4:00 p.m. I can no longer have a huge meal at 7:00 or 8:00 p.m. then sleep comfortably.

3. Another clue I'm getting older is like the time when I ran into some crusty geezer in a store, and he recognized me. He stopped to say hi then threw a memory at me, "Hey! Remember when we were on the school bus and Mrs. Houle almost got stuck when she was turning around at the bridge in Shady City? I thought you big kids were gonna hafta get out and push!" Comments like this twist my thoughts in so many directions. The fact that I believed he was an "old man" was quickly reshuffled in my brain's deck of cards. Then he had the nerve to call me one of the "big kids," obviously letting me know I was older than he was. Either my eyesight is worse than I thought, or maybe my mirrors need a good dusting.

4. I'm turning into my parents. I used to laugh at all the crazy, stupid, eye-rolling things they'd say or do. I'm sure they're the ones having the last laugh now as I walk out of a room and turn off the lights. Or maybe I'm channeling them when I turn the thermostat down a few degrees and put on a sweatshirt and

fuzzy socks. I remember snickering at my low electric bill one day as I stole an appreciative glance at my clothesline. And I still make soup out of whatever's left in the fridge after a week. The only rule is it can't be fuzzy or slimy.

5. I feel like I'm tempting The Fates or even spitting in Death's face when I buy green bananas. A very bold move, indeed!

6. I've become one of those GET OFF MY LAWN people. I like my lawn to be neat and precise. No trashy plastic decorations, no clumps of overgrown weeds, no unattended flower beds that got away from me, and definitely no junk vehicles.

7. I want more order and clean lines in my life now. Messes annoy me. This is probably a throwback to Ma's "Put it away NEATLY where it belongs!" days.

8. Noise bothers me. Maybe that's because I worked in a noisy environment for 34 years and finally have some silence to relish. I enjoy peace and quiet. They go together like coffee and chocolate, deck chairs and sunrises, Rocky and Adrian.

9. When I was young, I used to grab my car keys and wallet and hit the door. Now it's car keys, wallet, glasses, cell phone, tissues, an extra jacket, shopping bags, and lists. And don't forget to use the bathroom just before you leave.

10. My body doesn't want to move like it used to. What's up with THAT? How did I end up being so careful? Oh, I remember . . . that tumble that bumped my hip last year. I didn't break it, but I tapped it hard enough that it started the cartilage in my hip joint to start disintegrating, later resulting in a total hip replacement.

11. My memory is fading. Or maybe it's just a selective memory now. I do tend to write more things down, make lists, or leave visual cues to remind myself of whatever I wanted to do or needed to get. I blame this partly on retirement. When I was working, I had so much to remember all day, every day. Once I drove through that exit gate for the last time, it was like the

universe was giving me permission to be mentally lazy about remembering important items. If they're THAT important, I'll write 'em down now.

There you have it. Only a smattering of the many pieces of evidence that I'm getting old. I can't fight all of them. Hell, I actually EMBRACE a few things about getting older. In all fairness, let me give you the positives, the upside of the privilege of getting older.

1. I'm moving slower. As I mentioned above, my body doesn't want to move like it did when I was 20. And that's okay. Slowing down has its advantages. You get to see and enjoy what's around you so much more. Your attention is more focused on what's happening at the moment. If you're not flitting around, running from one thing to the next, you're given the opportunity to immerse yourself in the here and now. I used to take so much for granted. Now I look forward to the sunrise if I'm up early enough to catch it. Most evenings I'll lounge on my side deck and watch the sun go down. The colors seem more extraordinary as I get older. What I used to deem unimportant now takes precedence. The unworthy has turned into treasure.

2. Being prepared for emergencies for yourself is great. Being prepared for emergencies for others is even better. How many times have I pulled an unused tissue out of my jacket pocket for that harried mom standing in front of me at the checkout whose 3-year-old has a river of slimy snot pumping out of his nose? I've used my jumper cables that I carry in my car for more strangers than I have for myself. The jack knife I tote has cut tangled ropes, plastic tags, loose hem threads, and even big burgers. Never underestimate what an old woman carries in her purse. I think we're all secretly channeling MacGyver.

3. Not being around noise is a good thing. It gives me time to think, to ponder, to reflect. Without constant input clogging up my brain, I'm afforded the luxury of my own selfish thoughts.

Oh sure, I still have obligations and duties, but they're much more stripped down now. There's a lot to be said for simplicity.

4.   Another benefit of becoming "mature" is things naturally tend to roll off your back easier. You step away from drama and those who cause it. When someone starts stirring the pot, it's much easier to shrug, roll your eyes, and move on to something else that you prefer. You realize you do NOT have to subscribe to someone else's issues. It's liberating when you don't have to participate in another's petty antics.

5.   Saying NO is more acceptable as you get older. I touched on this topic in *Brain Scraps*, but it bears repeating. When we're young, we're expected to please others. We're trained to accept more work, more duties, more of whatever anyone wants to load upon our shoulders. As you get older, you finally develop an attitude that says you've had enough, and the door is closed. As that great philosopher Detective Harry Callahan used to say, "A man's got to know his limitations." So true! Know what your limitations are and don't let anyone push you any further than you're willing to go.

6. Getting older means you have more time to reflect on your past and if there are any mistakes or misdeeds that you can correct, you have the chance. We're all human and we all make mistakes. I've selfishly (in a good way) lightened my load of self-inflicted guilt. I've apologized to a couple of people who I thought deserved to hear it from me. The crazy part about this is that those people had totally forgotten about my slight or rudeness toward them. But I hadn't. For too long I'd carried the burden of guilt over an insensitive comment or deed. Once I made amends, I felt so much better. I'm sure there are people in my life with whom I'll never see eye-to-eye again, and that's fine. There are relationships that can't be fixed. Much like an old car that's way beyond repair, you just have to scrap it and get on with your life.

7. Aging is also good for the ego. It surprises and delights me when a younger person will call, text, or stop in and ask for my advice about something. There are a few life lessons I've learned these past 61 years or so, and I'm more than willing to share any tidbits of knowledge I have with others. It's something I appreciated when I was young and green. I was given some sound advice not only from my parents, but from neighbors, friends, and complete strangers. You can learn something from anyone, no matter what their age. Still, the wisest of them all are the old folks who have lived through most of what you have yet to encounter. Listen to these wise sages. Ask zillions of questions. Learn all you can from those of us in our golden years because sooner than you think, we won't be around. YOU will be the geezers in a blink of an eye.

8. Even with the subtle aches and pains of getting older, we're often reminded of what a gift that higher number can be. I think of all the friends and relatives I've known who passed on way too early. I've never had a problem with getting older. Aging IS a gift that is not given to all. There's no fair play, no equality in the age game. Some get to live to 100 years. Others are lucky to hit 100 hours. There are no guarantees, so it just drives it home how lucky we are to wake up every morning. I think age makes us appreciate how fast time goes and how there's nothing we can do to stop it.

There you have it. Evidence of my rank as Old Fart. I'm there and I'm embracing it because I can't turn back the hands of time, no matter how much I wish I could. I look forward to what the rest of my 60's will bring, I'll keep my fingers crossed for the gift of 70's, and if I'm really lucky and can beat the family genetic lottery, I might hit my 80's. I'll take it one shuffled step at a time and make sure I keep my eyes open for those sunsets.

MEET ME AT VIA MAIN

"Meet me at the Via Main restaurant," Carol requested. "I wanna run something by you." I'm always up for good food and excellent service, so of course I said yes. My friend Carol had been going through a rough time emotionally, so every now and then I'd send her an email to brighten her mood, make her laugh, or just get her mind off her troubles for a while. She especially loved it when I was on the midnight shift and a little punchy from sleep deprivation. She told me my sleep-deprived stories were always the best. Maybe it's because there's no filter when your body is running on auto. Anyone out there who has worked rotating shifts knows exactly what I'm talking about. This must be important if she can't talk over our emails, I thought.

I pulled my car into the Via Main's crowded parking lot and headed for the door. As I was about to grab the handle, an elderly gentleman beat me to it. "Allow me, young lady!" he said with a smile. His glossy dome looked freshly polished. He was wearing a T-shirt that had Man of the Year emblazoned on it in bold lettering. I instantly loved his attitude. I was in my 50's then, so being called "young lady" was a treat. I thanked him and waltzed into my favorite eatery. I looked around and saw the usual suspects. There was the retired State Trooper at the counter having breakfast. In the corner booth was the group of four women who enjoyed a leisurely breakfast at Via Main every morning. A few older gentlemen waved to my door opener as he scooted around me to claim his seat. A booth near the fireplace was open, so I slid onto the comfy seat and waited for Carol to arrive.

Carol and I are so much alike it's scary. If I'm not ten minutes early for an appointment, I consider myself late. I looked up and she was standing at the edge of the booth. "You beat me. AGAIN!" she started laughing. Carol nimbly placed her petite body on the booth bench opposite me. In her late 30's, Carol had a lot on her plate: mother to two kids, working full-time, keeping up with duties not only for her family, but for her husband's extensive family as well. Sometimes I wondered how she managed to squeeze an extra ten hours into each day. Maybe she had special powers. I could use those powers on vacations to make them last longer.

Diane Kennedy, the owner of the restaurant, came over to take our orders. Always smiling and with a kind word, Diane was a bright spot in everyone's day. We gave her our requests and off she scurried to the next table. Nobody could ever complain about the service at Diane's. Carol looked over at me with a serious look on her face. "I have something odd to tell you. I mentioned it to the hubby, but he just laughed at me. I told my mom, and she said I should look into mental health counseling." Carol rolled her eyes on her mother's comment. So did I. Carol is one of the most mentally stable people I know, so whatever she was about to tell me was going to be the truth and I knew it.

As our coffee was delivered, Carol started in on her story. I could tell she was agitated by her husband and mother, but there was something else niggling at her. "You know how sometimes a coincidence is JUST a coincidence? Any sane person would see the obvious and not read too much into any situation, right?" Her eyebrows went up a fraction, placing a slight wrinkle in her otherwise perfectly smooth face.

"Hey, you know me. I call those 'happy coincidences' in my life. I do believe sometimes things happen on their own. But then again, my mother taught me to NOT ignore any possible signs. Why? What's your coincidence?" I asked.

Carol sipped her coffee. Diane returned then with our omelets and toast so I dug in while Carol talked. "When I was a kid, we used to visit my grandfather near Malone. He had a wrap-around porch with a few chairs and a swing. He had a favorite rocking chair he always sat in and he'd constantly rock back and forth in it. He used to look up at the moon in the evenings in the summer. Gramps told me he'd rocked enough miles in that chair to make it to the moon and back."

I'd never met her grandfather, but I could picture him in my head. I only wish I'd had grandparents like that.

"I played him the Elton John song "Rocket Man" and he just loved it. From that time on, he'd call himself the Rocket (rock it) Man. He said that it was pretty nice of Elton to write a song about him." Too funny.

"So, what's this have to do with anything? I know you miss your grandfather since he passed away last year." Some deaths weigh heavier than others, and I knew this one weighed a ton on her.

"He wanted me to have his rocking chair when he died. It's been wonderful having it in the house, but it's bittersweet. Remembering him rocking me in that chair when I was a kid floods my heart with such good memories. He held and rocked both of my kids in that chair, too." A couple of tears welled up in Carol's eyes as she remembered those moments with her grandfather. "And this is why I wanted to talk to you. I wanted to see what you thought of what's been happening at home. Maybe I'm nuts. Maybe I'm imagining things because I miss him so much." She slathered peanut butter onto her toast and took a big bite.

"If whatever is happening brings you comfort, then just accept it. You don't have to prove anything to anyone. Now, if you're really going off the deep end, don't worry. You have enough people around you who will reel you in and make sure you're fine." I can't stand it when people are so dismissive of another's questionable events. Hey, if you weren't there, don't judge.

"Last Wednesday was his birthday. Gramps would have been 79. I went home for lunch as usual. I walked in, flipped the kitchen light on, and turned the radio on to hear the local news. The kids were in school, Bob was at work, and there wasn't anyone else in the house. We don't even have pets because of Bob's allergies, so I can't blame a dog or cat. I was getting my food ready and glanced into the living room for a second. I don't know why, but I felt like someone was in there. And you know how my house is set up. There's nowhere for anyone to hide in the living room. Still, I thought for sure someone was in there, but the weird thing is I wasn't afraid." Carol gave a little shrug then continued, "I looked at that rocking chair and said, 'Happy birthday, Gramps. I miss you,' and that's when it happened. His chair started rocking ever so slightly. It was more than just a little movement. It was definitely moving back and forth more than a few times. More like eight or ten times it went back and forth." Carol's eyes went big. She stared straight into mine. I smiled and gave her a small nod.

"Are you actually surprised? I mean, really? You and your Gramps were pretty close. You miss him something awful. Why wouldn't he let you know he's still around and wanted to say hi?" I think my acceptance of her incident relieved her. Carol's face softened slightly.

"You're right. Why wouldn't he?" Carol mused. "But here's the really cool part. And I KNOW it's just a coincidence, but . . ." her voice trailed off for a few seconds. "But then the radio started playing Elton John's "Rocket Man" and I jumped. As soon as I heard the first few words of that song, I started crying and laughing at the same time. I went over to the radio and I cranked it. I walked to the rocking chair, sat down, and belted out ROCKET MANNNNNNN! I felt so much better after that. Bob and my mom think I'm losing it. They think I'm nuts. But I know what I saw and heard." Carol's wide eyes and smile were lighting up her pretty face.

"I'm tickled you didn't ignore his sign. Please keep letting your gramps and anyone else who has passed know you're still thinking of them," I said. Carol promised me she would.

We had finished our delicious breakfast and Diane came over to pick up our plates. She put two to-go boxes in front of us, each containing a piece of cake. "I couldn't help overhearing about your grandfather," she said to Carol. "I just wanted to wish him a happy birthday, too!" And with that glowing smile, off she went again to make her corner of the world a better place.

I love it. I really do LOVE this stuff. Say what you will, but not all coincidences are just that. Sometimes they ARE messages. Now and then, there isn't an explanation. For those naysayers who tell me I read too much into everything, I say so what? I'm not going to take the chance of ignoring my dead people. I know they look out for us, so it's just common courtesy to let them know we appreciate their gestures. I still see Carol now and then and we keep in touch on social media quite often. She's still getting messages from her gramps, and they comfort her. She tells me about her latest "what ifs" and likes to hear what I think of them. I told her I'm jealous she had . . . and still has . . . such a wonderful gramps.

UNCLE JOE

My mother had two brothers: Lee and Joe. I've already written a chapter about Uncle Lee, so now it's Uncle Joe's turn. Uncle Joe's real name was Harold Asel Thomas, Junior, but everyone called him Joe. My grandparents had given him that nickname after seeing their son enjoy the 1938 cartoon character Injun Joe. I'm sure it was easier than specifying Harold Senior or Harold Junior when it came time to call out for one of them. Only family and friends knew the younger Harold as Joe. For obvious reasons, Joe dropped his middle name when he went into the Army as a teen. He said it sounded too much like . . . well . . . you can figure that out.

When he became a security guard for Pinkerton, and later for the New York Power Authority, he went by Harold. Uncle Joe did this for a reason. If he was home on his day off and the phone rang (before the days of caller I.D.), his wife Hilda would answer. If the person asked for Harold, she'd say sorry, he's not home. If they asked for Joe, she'd hand the phone over to him. Pretty good plan until years later when I was hired at the Power Authority and I slipped and called him Uncle Joe. People found out he went by "Joe" after hours, so once in a while a boss would call and ask for "Joe." Oops. Sorry, Uncle Joe!

Uncle Joe was number five out of six children. My mother was born four years after Joe, so she was the baby of the family. There was one more after my mother, but she was stillborn, so Rosalee Dawn never made her mark in this world. (Years later my mother would say it was that name that killed her.) As with most siblings, there was always squabbling, fighting, and constant annoyances between them. No matter how strict my grandparents were, there would always be a poke here, a bump there, or maybe just verbal sparring between the kids.

These stories about Uncle Joe come mostly from my mother's point of view. Both she and her brother have long since died, so there's nobody to vouch for the veracity of her claims. Being the baby of the family, I'm sure her opinions and recollections may have been slightly skewed. Still, they make me laugh whenever I think of them. For instance, my mother remembered being slightly pudgy as a child. She used to walk from the family home on Hubbard Road in Massena over to the elementary school on Brighton Street. Uncle Joe would walk with her and chant, "Porky Pig is nice and big. Porky Pig is nice and big," to the cadence of her short footsteps. Big brothers are always thorough at humiliating and embarrassing younger siblings. Uncle Joe had his big brother routine down pat. Because my mother was slightly round, he nicknamed her Porky or just Pork for short. My mother adored her brother, even when he was being rotten to her. Such is life as a sibling. You only-child people will never know the torment of being one of many.

One day while Uncle Joe and my mother were outside, he looked down at her and said, "Hey Pork! I bet I can piss higher than you can on the garage wall." Well, my five-year-old mother was never one to back down from a bet or a dare. She wanted to prove she was just as good as her big brother, so she took that bet. He said he'd go first and asked her to turn away for a minute. He then shielded his privates and proceeded to spray a long, wide arc on the side of the garage.

He put his tool away, then said, "Okay, Pork, your turn! See if you can beat that!"

Porky . . . um . . . I mean Marilyn looked up at his impressive urine half-moon on the dry wood. "Ha! I can beat that," she thought. She dropped her pants and underwear, stuck her chubby belly out as far as she could, and proceeded to piss down both legs into her undies, pants, socks, and shoes. Uncle Joe started laughing and told her she lost the bet. By this time my mother was crying. She was tearful not only because he was laughing at her, but because she'd lost the bet. The worst part was she actually thought she could spray a stream just by pointing her girly bits in the right direction. Ah, the innocence and stupidity of the young. Marilyn pulled up her soaked undies and pants and ran sloshing into the house. Through her tears, she told her father what her big brother had just done. Harold Senior went outside and invited Harold Junior to the woodshed. Uncle Joe always said watching his little sister wet herself was worth the swats from their dad.

As my mother became a little older, she honed her conniving skills. One day she was in the kitchen making toast. Uncle Joe was sitting at the table reading the newspaper. Out of the blue, Marilyn started crying, "OW! OW! STOP IT, JOE! STOP HITTING ME! OWW!" Uncle Joe looked up quizzically at her and that's when their father came storming into the kitchen. My mother had pushed herself into a corner with her arms up protecting her face. Uncle Joe was finally getting it. Senior grabbed Junior and marched him out to the woodshed. Again. On his way out, he glanced at his rotten little sister as she was wiggling her fingers and tongue at him, smiling the whole time. He eventually retaliated, but she claimed the look on his face when their dad grabbed him was priceless.

Then there was the time when Marilyn was about 10 or so and Joe was about 14. He came to the table and sat down for supper. Everyone stared at him because he'd shaved all of the hair on his head and eyebrows completely off. I mean smooth. No stubble whatsoever. His father quietly asked what happened. Joe replied that a girl in school informed him if he shaved his hair off, it would grow back in thick and curly. Everyone loves thick, curly hair, right? His parents just shook their heads and ate their supper. The next night Uncle Joe and my mother were at the table first and before either of their parents could see him, he reached down and picked up his fork. He then gave Marilyn an evil grin and lightly scratched his bald head. Marilyn rolled her eyes, but then he pointed to HER fork and scratched his head again. He was letting her know he'd scratched his shiny, bald pate with HER fork. The crying began. "MOM! JOE SCRATCHED HIS HEAD WITH MY FORK!" Both parents then turned to look at Uncle Joe seated at the table. He gave them an "I don't know what the Hell she's talking about" look. He must have been convincing, because neither parent yelled at him. They just looked at my mother and told her to calm down and start eating. Every now and then Uncle Joe would look up from his plate and just smile at my mother. She said she had a hard time eating with her fork that night.

For the record, Uncle Joe did have beautiful hair, but it was baby-fine and straight. He had no curls, even after it all grew back in. I can definitely vouch for his eyebrows, though. When I was about 12, whenever he'd visit us at the farm, I'd trim the wild hairs growing out of his eyebrows. I used to call them his feelers. I told him he looked like a big bug and asked if I could pluck the long stray hairs. He said yes for the first one, but once he found out how much it hurt to use tweezers to pluck a hair out, he said I could only use scissors after that. And that was my job when he came to visit. I'd snip those four-inch feelers from his eyebrows. He'd never had daughters, so he took my word for it when I told him he "had" to let me trim his eyebrows. He indulged me as any good uncle would.

I think my fondest memory of Uncle Joe was what he did every October 26th. As I mentioned, he was my mother's brother. He had the same birthday as my father, but Oscar was one year older. We moved up here in April 1974. Starting in October 1974, Uncle Joe would come out to the farm early in the morning to "help" my father with morning chores. His six-foot-two frame lumbered in at 5:00 a.m. as my father was having a cup of coffee and getting his boots on to head to the barn. Uncle Joe would stomp all through the house waking everyone else up. "IT'S DAYLIGHT IN THE SWAMP! C'MON! IT'S TIME FOR CHORES! EVERYONE UP!" He'd be laughing his ass off as he hooted and hollered to get everyone out of bed at 5:00 a.m. A couple of times it was on a school day, so he'd tell us kids if we weren't going to help with chores, at least we'd be up in time to catch the bus. Funny guy. Yeah. After a couple of years of 5:00 a.m. visits, Uncle Joe decided he needed to wake OSCAR up for birthday chores. He started coming out at 4:00 a.m. He'd open the back door into the kitchen slightly, then kick it hard so it would swing open fast and hit our big metal garbage can sitting behind it. He'd start hollering as he entered the kitchen, his deep voice carried through to my parents' downstairs bedroom and to us kids in our rooms upstairs. "RISE AND SHINE! IT'S OUR BIRTHDAY, OSCAR! LET'S GO PULL SOME TITS!" My mother had a few choice words for her big brother who was still, after all those years, tormenting her. My father just laughed and turned the coffee pot on to start the day.

I always admired Uncle Joe for many reasons. A handsome man with brilliant blue eyes, and a slender physique, he was a heartbreaker for sure. He enlisted in the Army right out of high school. Uncle Joe was a career man and served his country proudly. He was typical of the men of that era who could fix anything and, even if it wasn't the prettiest outcome, it would work. He built bookshelves for my mother in our dining room. I still remember him jumping up on them and swinging from one of the 2x4 dividers. Those bookshelves weren't going anywhere. Ever. His concrete skills made me wonder if he'd ever sent anyone to swim with the fishes. Uncle Joe worked hard all his life, provided a comfortable home for his wife and three sons, and helped anyone who asked. Sadly, cancer took him at the young age of 59. He barely had any time to enjoy his retirement and, for that, I'm bitter on his behalf. Anyone who works hard should be able to enjoy their "golden years."

Every October 26th I still perk up my ears early in the morning waiting and hoping to hear "IT'S DAYLIGHT IN THE SWAMP!" I know Uncle Joe is gone, but part of me still wishes I could hear that door being kicked in just one more time. What I wouldn't give to hear his voice hollering for us to stop being lazy and to get out of bed. And every year I have a piece of cake or pie in honor of my uncle and my father on their special day.

ALL'S FAIR WITH OSCAR

Way back in the 1960's we lived on a modest dairy farm down near Albion, NY. My father was known for being an excellent herdsman and his knowledge of dairy cows was widely respected in the farming community. Every summer Oscar would select his best registered Holstein cows and heifers to take to the county fair. A couple of times he even took Big Dan, our breeding bull. Coming home with the coveted blue ribbons was a common outcome for Oscar. He worked hard at raising the best quality dairy cows possible and it showed.

Around this time, the folks made friends with Herb and June Genagon (pronounced jenna-john). They had a son by the name of Ted who was about fifteen years younger than Oscar. Ted looked up to my father like a favorite uncle. Oscar spent time doing what he loved best: teaching about dairy cattle. Ted was an eager student who absorbed every bit of knowledge Oscar imparted.

One year during fair season, Ted asked his parents if he could go with Oscar to show his cattle. His folks said, "Sure!" They trusted Oscar and knew Ted was in good hands.

One hot summer evening my father led a cow out to the wash rack. Ted followed behind with another cow. When Oscar was done cleaning the first one, he handed her off to Ted and said, "Ted, take her in, tie her up, and grab the next cow. And bring us a couple of cold beers." Hey, it was a hot night and the two guys were working hard getting those cows spiffed up for the show ring!

Ted dutifully did what Oscar asked. He took the clean cow inside the barn, snagged a couple of cold beers from the cooler, and untied the next cow to be taken to the wash rack. Oscar treated Ted like a man and Ted appreciated it. Oscar also knew Ted was only 15 and probably didn't have much, if any, drinking experience. Guess what, Ted? Today's the day.

Cow after cow came out and went in. With each turn-around came two more beers for the hard-working men. After about the sixth cow, Oscar was waiting at the wash rack. No Ted. Oscar chuckled to himself. He walked into the barn and there, on a stack of hay, was Ted. He was sprawled out and snoring. Oscar smirked, shook his head, covered Ted with a blanket, and went back outside with another cow.

The next morning Ted's folks showed up bright and early. They found Ted still sleeping on the bales of hay. He was still snuggled under the blanket and not in anyone's path. When Herb and June looked down at their slumbering son, they asked Oscar why he was still sleeping. It was past 7:00 a.m. so why wasn't he up and helping with the cows? Oscar looked them straight in the eye and told them what a great job Ted had been doing. He told them Ted had stayed up all night long removing the manure from the cows' stalls so they wouldn't get dirty before showtime. Oh, how proud Ted's folks were of their son!

Eventually Ted woke up and found Oscar. He had a bit of a headache and a queasy stomach. Other than that, he felt fine. He asked if his parents had shown up yet and Oscar said yes. Ted's face drained of color. He figured he'd be getting hell from his parents for drinking and passing out. At only age 15! But no. Oscar told him how happy and proud his parents were that Ted had taken the initiative to keep the cows clean all night long. Ted looked at Oscar in disbelief and cracked a smile. Herb and June never knew the truth.

* * * * *

Another Oscar/Ted story at one of the fairs was about the bull. Big Dan was a monster of a bull. Of course, I saw him through a child's eyes. To me he looked about the size of a well-fed elephant, but in real life I'm sure he was an average Holstein bull. Big Dan had an impressive pedigree and a more impressive physique. It always impressed me the way my father could handle that magnificent beast with just two fingers in his nose ring. (And, yes, when I see these kids today with nose rings, I have to fight the urge to put my index and middle fingers in the ring and lead that person around!) This one particular time Oscar was prepping Big Dan for the ring. Ted was helping him get Big Dan washed, brushed, and looking good. Big Dan, however, must have noticed all the lovely ladies in their stalls around the barn and wanted to do a bit of romancing. His mind was NOT on cooperating with Oscar. That's when Oscar asked Ted to grab some beer. Ted had a look of "OH NO!" on his face. He vividly remembered what happened the last time Oscar mentioned beer. Oscar laughed and said it was for the bull, not him. Ted went to the cooler and brought back several bottles of Genesee beer. Oscar popped the cap off a bottle, grabbed Big Dan around his massive neck and chin, and proceeded to pour the beer down the bull's throat. Big Dan liked it. Ted handed Oscar the second bottle. After about seven bottles of beer, Big Dan was starting to mellow out. His body looked a little fuller but not bloated. Oscar put his two fingers into Big Dan's nose ring and walked him quietly to the show tent. The mighty Big Dan was led by Oscar around the ring as if he were a baby lamb. No bellowing, no pulling, no locked legs. Just the biggest docile creature to ever grace the sawdust covered floor. Oscar and Big Dan walked away with the blue ribbon, of course.

Fast forward many years later. We moved up here in 1974 but Ted still lived down in western New York. The folks kept in touch with Ted even after his parents had died. Then my mother passed in 2002. Ted decided he needed to come visit Oscar, so some time around 2005 or so he began making the trip up here once a year to see Oscar. Oscar appreciated Ted's efforts and always enjoyed reliving their glory days of their adventures and shenanigans at the county fairs. Eventually Oscar ended up in a nursing home, but Ted would send pictures of cows, tractors, and the fairs he still attended downstate. Ted kept up his yearly visits. Before Alzheimer's took complete control over Oscar's mind, he made us kids promise to ask Ted to do his eulogy. Oscar knew what was happening to him. Alzheimer's runs in his family as deep and wide as the Mississippi River. We promised we'd have Ted say the last words.

In October of 2013, one day after Oscar's 82nd birthday, he passed. It was a relief to see he was finally set free of that unrelenting bastard of a disease. Sure enough, Ted drove up to give Oscar's eulogy, and what a send-off it was! Bless Ted's heart, he had everyone in stitches at Oscar's funeral. He relayed the cow washing incident and how his parents never knew about the beer, not even in their dying days. He described in detail what a semi-drunk bull looks like and how he handles in the show ring. Ted told so many Oscar stories that he brought tears of laughter to everyone's eyes. And that's exactly why Oscar wanted Ted to have the last words.

I had kept in touch with Ted for the years following Oscar's death. We'd exchange an email here and there and the odd Facebook message or post. Every year on Oscar's birthday Ted would call and retell those famous stories. Then, one day I opened Facebook and saw his granddaughter had posted that Ted had passed. He'd had a head injury and didn't recover. My heart sank. I hadn't chatted with Ted in several months and I took for granted he'd always be there. He was the strongest connection I had with my father, and I cherished hearing all of those stories over and over again. And now they are done. Finished.

After I read Ted's granddaughter's post, I closed my laptop and went out on my front deck. It was early in the morning. It was quiet. looked up and said, "Ted, I'm sorry I didn't get to say good-bye to you. If you can hear me, I want to thank you for always being so kind to Oscar and always being there for him. You were more than a friend. You were part of our family and I'll miss you. I hope you found Oscar up there and I hope you're reliving your county fair stories. Just watch out for those bottles of Genny!" And just then, for the first time ever, a dragonfly landed on my hand. It sat there on my finger for a good minute. I had my cell phone next to me and slowly lifted it and took a few pictures. I'd NEVER had a dragonfly land on me. Never. Until that day. And I haven't had one land on me since. I laughed. I cried. I then thanked Ted for letting me know he found Oscar and they're having a riot up there.

OSTRANDER GRAVE

If you read *Brain Scraps*, you may remember the story of our haunted mansion down in western New York. If you missed that story or need a quick refresher, here it is in a nutshell: The Ostrander family that owned the house many years before us had a mentally challenged child they kept locked away in a room up in the third-floor attic. That house was definitely haunted, and we experienced many odd events including heavy breathing when nobody else was in the room, cold spots, blue orbs appearing then just as quickly disappearing. We were chased down the stairways by . . . nobody. Or shall I say no body? And, of course, the sound of a baby crying was common. Friends of the family witnessed many of these happenings, so we know we weren't imagining them.

As mentioned before, the Ostranders were extremely intelligent people. Having a mentally challenged child was considered an embarrassment way back in the olden times. They weren't as enlightened or understanding as we are today. This is where my story about that child picks up from *Brain Scraps*. Let me pull a Paul Harvey on you and give you The Rest of the Story.

My mother was curious as to what happened to that special child. She scoured public records. She checked with birth and death registers. Back then there was no internet, so everything had to be looked up in old newspapers or public records that were kept in archives. Mickey dug for the truth. My mother wanted to know what happened to this child in the room in the big attic. Did he grow up to adulthood? Did he die as a child? Did he get moved to some kind of institution? Eventually my mother came across the death records for the Ostranders. No mention anywhere of a dead son, whether as a child or as an adult. She did, however, find out where the family burial plot was located.

One spring day while we kids were in school and Oscar was at work, Mickey took a little road trip. It wasn't very far, but definitely not on her usual route to get groceries or do other household errands. That day she put gloves, a shovel, a crowbar, and a long metal pigtail fence post in the old station wagon and headed out to a spot on her road map. She didn't really know what she was going to need or use, so she figured a variety of implements would do the trick. When Mickey arrived at the old cemetery, it didn't take long to find the Ostrander graves. There was a tall monument marking the family plot, and several smaller stones around it. There was a low, black wrought iron fence surrounding the graves. Nobody had tended to the last resting spots of the Ostranders in decades.

Mickey looked around and it was obvious this was not a well-traveled area. She knew what she was about to do was probably illegal or at the very least frowned upon by most people. But she HAD to know. No, she did NOT dig up the graves. Please give her a little more credit than that. The first thing my mother did was ask permission of any lingering spirits if she could do some checking on the graves. I realize this sounds silly, but it doesn't hurt to show respect to the dead. When a lightning bolt didn't hit her, she took that as permission to go ahead with her plan. She then took that long pigtail fence post and started methodically poking the ground. She started at the graves with the latest dates on them. She eased the metal rod down into the ground about three feet and when it didn't hit anything, she moved it over one foot and tried it again. She did this with several graves. Same result every time: nothing. Finally, she came to the mother's grave. She started at the headstone and pushed the pigtail down and at approximately two feet deep, she felt resistance. She heard a hollow "thunk" when she tapped the rod downward. Mick raised the rod and moved it over one foot.

Pressing the soil, the metal made another hollow thunk at about the same depth as the first poke. Mickey moved down, heading toward the foot of the grave, but going in one-foot increments each time. Perhaps the stories she'd heard from the old timers in the neighborhood were true. The rumor among some old folks was that the child who was kept in the attic lived into his 30's. By then, his mother had died and was buried in the family plot. When the boy died, he was quietly buried on top of his mother, in the same grave. Poke. Poke. Poke. By the time my mother was finished poking the ground on Mrs. Ostrander's grave, she had covered an area approximately two feet wide and six feet long and nothing more than two feet deep.

Just for curiosity's sake, Mickey walked around to other random graves in the cemetery and started checking them out too. None of the other graves stopped her pigtail rod at less than three feet deep. No matter which ones she tried, they all went deep into the ground. The only grave that produced that shallow thudding noise was the Ostrander matriarch's.

My mother walked back to that one particular grave that she had invaded so thoroughly. She bowed her head and said, "Little guy, I know you existed. You are not forgotten. Rest in peace."

DESERVE

I'm a softy. Truly, I am. I've also been called gullible, easily duped, and a pushover. I can't deny any of those charges. It's just my nature to give people not only a second chance, but a third, fourth, and even more because deep down I really want to believe that people are good. We all have moments when we're not at our best. We screw up. The wrong words come out of our mouths. Promises aren't fulfilled. Being human can be so tough at times, and I know I'm far from perfect. I overlook way too much in others because I DO see the good in people, even the ones who seem to go out of their way to be idiots!

This trusting attitude has caused me immeasurable heartaches over the years. It's cost me money and, at times, my sanity. And yet I still open my arms and trust others. What's the definition of insanity? Yup, you remember. Doing the same thing over and over again and expecting different results. Still, I can't be a cynic. I won't be a naysayer and automatically have my guard up when I meet new people. I probably should be more cautious, but again, that's just not my nature. I'm way too trusting and have been taken advantage of by some pretty awful users out there. Deep in my heart I believe in karma, and I hope someday those people will get what's coming to them.

One of the many things my mother taught me was to never wish anything bad on anyone because it'll boomerang on you. It'll come back to you tenfold. She was more in tune with the universe than anyone else I ever knew. She taught me when it comes to others, no matter if they're sweet and kind or if they're nasty and evil, always wish the same for them: always ask the universe for them to get what they deserve. That's a powerful word. Deserve. Ma explained it this way: the universe (or higher being, whatever you prefer), likes balance. If you wish something bad on someone who has done you wrong, you're just piling more negativity on top of an already bad situation. Hmmm. Very true. On the flip side, if you put it out there for only good things to happen to someone who truly deserves a break, isn't that the right thing to do? Now back to those nasty, selfish people. Suppose they're just plain cruel, selfish, manipulative and so on. I think we're all programmed to want revenge. After all, aren't most movies and books about getting even? Isn't there a delicious thrill in watching someone get their comeuppance? We all eagerly watch as the bad guy gets his ass kicked or when the mean girl gets humiliated in front of a crowd. There's a divine righteousness in our souls. We want to see balance. We yearn for fairness, so what's wrong with wishing bad things on bad people? Won't that make things even? No. Not even close.

I'm just as guilty as the next person when it comes to wanting revenge. Or maybe to at least sit back and watch someone who has done me wrong have a bit of misfortune. Call me petty. I'm not above it and never will be. There's that damned human thing again. I don't wish death or serious illnesses on anyone. Ever. But I wouldn't object if the universe dished out a few flat tires or missed flights on my behalf. If the universe wants to throw in a leaky pipe or incontinent dog here and there, I'd be amenable to those ideas. The weird thing with me is, for just a split second I almost feel guilty when I hear about these things happening to someone who has irked me. For a wee moment in time, I wonder if I caused someone else's unfortunate events just by wishing for them to get what they deserved. Seriously? Aw, c'mon. I don't have that kind of power. Or do I? If I feel fine about wishing good things for good people and something wonderful happens to them, can I take the credit? HA! Probably not. Still, isn't it a delightful idea thinking we have any control over destiny? How is this idea of "wishing you get what you deserve" any different from prayer? Is it the same thing? Aren't prayers just wishes we send up for ourselves or others? Or are they only prayers when they're filled with good intentions? Probably.

It's difficult to not wish for disaster to happen to someone who has hurt you. It's extremely hard to hold in that rage and anger. Getting even is like taking a bath. The hot water feels so good for a little while, but after a bit it gets cold, and you have to get out of it. As I said, I don't ever wish anything bad on anyone, I only wish they get what they deserve. And sometimes I win. That's how it feels to me. Somehow, I feel justified in my haughty attitude when I hear about the universe making things even. I admit I smirk just a little bit when I hear about that flat tire or pet-stained carpet. I also grin and giggle when I find out something wonderfully positive happened for a friend who really deserved it. Then I sit back and wonder . . . who is grinning when I have those awful incidents in my life? Who is smirking because I took a spill or because something didn't work out for me? What goes around comes around, right? My imperfections make me human. They make sure I commit my fair share of mistakes. I've given it some thought and have decided to try to deny anyone that sweet feeling of getting even. Maybe, just maybe if I try to be a little nicer, a bit more forgiving, and a little less judgmental, there won't be too many people salivating at the chance to see me fall or fail. Perhaps that's the key to this insanity. If I hope others get what they deserve, then it's only fair that I wish for the same for myself. Hoo-boy. I'd better straighten up then. I have my work cut out for me. Wish me luck!

A REASON

"Everything happens for a reason." That old axiom used to get to me. My mother used it way too many times when something crappy happened and there wasn't any explanation. I like things neat and tidy. I like stories finished, wrapped up, completed. When something unfair or totally uncalled for would happen, I'd whine about it and my mother would throw that useless "Everything happens for a reason" at me. I'd get upset and snap back, "But that's not FAIR!" Again, she'd toss another one of her favorite sayings at me, "Life is rarely fair." ARRRGGHHH!!!

I'd come to despise those two sayings. I wanted answers and explanations for the rotten things that happened to me, my family, my friends. Funny thing is, I never asked why any of the GOOD things happened. In my selfish young mind, I only saw the negatives. I rarely took notice of the everyday blessings bestowed upon me or the others in my world. Typical kid, eh? Never once did I think *gee, this has been a wonderful year for hay. My folks won't have to pay through the nose for a hundred bales of sub-par hay to get the cows through the winter.* Never crossed my mind to say thank you when the school bus came along to pick me up and take me to a place of learning. Many people in this world aren't afforded an education. Did I say a thank you to the Garden Gods when our bountiful land produced tons of string beans, cucumbers, tomatoes? Nope. Selfish, blind child that I was, none of those things ever crossed my radar.

Swede (the same dog who helped Oscar in the kitchen in *Brain Scraps*), was our beautiful 200-pound St. Bernard who thought she was a lap dog. No matter where you were sitting, she'd come over and lean into you then slide onto your body as if you were designed to hold her enormous furry carcass. Everybody loved that gigantic teddy bear of a dog. One day a couple of our friends were visiting the farm and the gal, Debbie, asked if she could take Swede for a walk. She was always delighted by how well the dog obeyed and didn't even need a leash. Debbie and Swede headed down our empty country road. Then Debbie decided she wanted to go check out the bridge on what we called the main road, which is now known as County Route 55. That road is much busier as travelers head from North Lawrence to Helena or the other way around. On that particular late afternoon, as Debbie was walking our St. Bernard toward the bridge, a car came lumbering up behind her. Debbie turned and immediately stepped off the side of the road toward the guardrail. Unfortunately, Swede did not. She was on the edge of the road, but that didn't matter. The car smashed into our beloved Swede right in front of Debbie's eyes. The driver of the car didn't even stop. Probably another useless, selfish drunk driver. Debbie freaked out and ran back to the farm to get my father. Oscar and my brother Tyler hopped in the pickup truck. They went toward the bridge, and there was our magnificent dog mangled on the side of the road. She was dead. No question about it. My father and brother picked up Swede's lifeless body and placed her gently into the bed of the truck and drove her home. We were all standing outside in the driveway when Oscar pulled in and put the truck in park.

As we gathered around the still body of our best friend, we started crying. All of us. That dog was the most gentle, loving creature ever put on this earth. If I hear anyone saying, "It was just a dog," I feel like biting them myself. There's NO SUCH THING as "just" a dog. This was a member of our family. And now she is gone.

I couldn't stand there any longer listening to Debbie apologize for what was not her fault. She felt terribly guilty and responsible for Swede's death. We all assured her it wasn't her fault, but how could any decent person not feel the pang of guilt? With a heavy heart, I turned and went back inside the house. I needed a good gut-wrenching cry, so I headed upstairs to my room to scream into my pillow. This definitely was not fair.

As I hit the top of the stairs, I was about to turn left and go into the room I shared with one of my sisters. Off to the right, on the other side of the room the stairway opened into, was my brother's room. I could distinctly hear an odd noise coming from Tyler's room. Sort of like loud static from a radio, but I knew he didn't have a radio in there. We were taught to always respect other people's privacy, so I hollered downstairs, "Hey Tyler! What's going on in your bedroom? I hear something!"

Tyler came to the foot of the stairs. "What are you talking about? I'm not doing anything there!" Up the stairs he went, frustrated with me for being nosy and pulling him away from what was happening with our dog.

Tyler trudged to his door and threw it open wide to show me nothing was going on in his room. At that moment, we both saw the end wall of his room was ON FIRE. The fuse box was in there and somehow it had caught fire and the old, dry boards were burning like campfire tinder. We ran down the stairs screaming, "THE HOUSE IS ON FIRE! THE HOUSE IS ON FIRE!"

We all started grabbing buckets of water and hauling them upstairs as my mother called the fire department. When it was obvious our buckets of water weren't enough to do the trick, Oscar pushed us all out of the house to wait for the firemen. He grabbed a small stack of paperwork he deemed important and carried that out and placed it in the cab of the truck. (We later realized it was the deed to the farm.)

The local fire departments came but unfortunately overshot the house assuming it was the barn that was on fire. All of us were running down our one-lane road asking the gawkers and looky-loos to PLEASE back up! BACK UP! The firetrucks couldn't get to the house because these nosy people wanted to SEE the gore. I have never hated people so much as I did at that moment. Our home was burning and these people sat in their cars staring at the flames. FINALLY, we had enough cars backed up or pulled off to the side of the road that the firetrucks could get to the house. They did a fantastic job containing the fire to only Tyler's bedroom and that part of the roof. Most of the damage was water damage as it flowed down to the bottom floor. All of the pictures on the walls were ruined. Curtains were sooty and wet. The floors were spongy.

But we were alive.

How is all this tied together? Well, I will believe until my dying day that Swede saved us. If Swede hadn't been killed at that very moment, I wouldn't have gone upstairs to cry my eyes out. I wouldn't have heard that odd sound coming from Tyler's room. The way the house was cut up, Tyler's room was at the furthest end of the house. As a family, we used to spend most of our time in the kitchen. We didn't usually hang out in the living room until in the evening, after chores were done so we could watch one of our two channels. PBS or the Montreal station. Oh boy.

I know we would have lost the whole house if that precious dog hadn't been taken from us on that fateful day. Her death saved our home. Nothing and nobody will ever convince me otherwise.

This was one of those rare moments I was given the gift of knowing the WHY. I could have been angry and bitter over losing our sweet dog. Instead, I thanked her for sacrificing herself and protecting us, just like any good dog would do.

DO AS I SAY,
NOT AS I DO

How many times did I hear THAT expression? My parents tried. They really did. Alas, they were only human and made mistakes like everyone else. This essay is a little bit funny, and a little bit sad. And yet, it's the bare truth, too, so take from it what you will.

I vividly remember my mother lighting up another cigarette and when one of us would ask if we could smoke too, she'd snap, "Do as I say, not as I do!" She'd then ramble on about how terrible smoking was for you, how it costs a lot of money, it's a nasty habit, and so on. Her hypocrisy made us angry. Not that we WANTED to get lung cancer as small children, but we wanted the option. After all, smoking was SO grown up. In the end, two of my brothers did become smokers. It was a double standard in our home. The boys were allowed to do pretty much anything they wanted. My mother justified her leniency by saying she'd rather have them smoking safely in front of her than hiding in the barn and setting the haymow on fire. Smoking at home and allowing my brothers to do it openly was one of my mother's and father's biggest regrets in life. They often chastised themselves for setting such a bad example and for pretty much saying hey, it's okay to kill yourself. What loving parent actually encourages detrimental habits and addictions in their own children? At first, it's sort of cool that your kid is like you but then you realize the idiotic thing you've done. Even though both of my parents eventually quit the tobacco habit, the damage was already done with two of their boys.

With the exception of cigarette smoking (both parents) and cigar smoking (just my father), the folks didn't really have too many bad habits to instill in their six children. We all learned their fierce work ethic. Each one of us knew how to be frugal and stretch a penny. None of us wasted a thing if we could help it. For the most part I believe we were kind to people and helped others when we could. See? Plenty of good things were taught that carried through to our adult lives. So far, so good! Looking back now, I recall a few funny moments where that old "Do as I say, not as I do" comes into play. For instance . . .

That time my mother was sick and tired of seeing a certain pop star's picture in the tabloids. He'd dramatically changed his looks through multiple plastic surgeries until he was unrecognizable. A tabloid held a look-alike contest and one night after a couple of adult beverages, my mother thought it would be funny to send in a Polaroid picture of her bare buttocks. A few weeks afterward, the tabloid did print the winner and my mother was disappointed to see she hadn't won. She did, however, snicker when she read a line in the article about how some people sent in unprintable photos and they did not resemble the pop star at all. It was a couple of years after that when this same pop star was busted for molesting children and paying off their parents. Maybe my mother wasn't so far off after all. Still, lesson learned: Don't send pics of your butt to anyone. (And this was LONG before cell phones had been invented!)

Another thing my mother taught me: Never put Vaseline in your hair. She thought she'd pull a funny one on us. My brother was still in high school, and I was out on my own, but going to the farm for supper that night. When I walked into the house, I saw she'd slathered Vaseline on her hair and pulled it up into a point on the top of her head like Martin Short's character Ed Grimley on SCTV. I lost it. My little brother Tim was just getting off the school bus and when he walked in, he just shook his head. "What's WRONG with you?" he asked while laughing.

"I'm Ed Grimley from TV!" she exclaimed. She'd pulled her

pants up high, had her shirt buttoned up to her neck, and her hair looked like an exclamation point on the top of her head.

We all laughed and agreed she nailed it. Too funny. Tim then went to his bedroom to change his clothes and Ma went to the bathroom sink to wash her hair. That's when we heard laughing. It was Ma and she was really losing it. She came out of the bathroom with a towel around her shoulders and her hair sticking out in all directions.

"I thought you were going to wash your hair?" I asked.

"I was, but . . . but . . . apparently Vaseline d-d-does NOT come out w-w-with shampoo!" Ma hysterically sputtered. She was laughing so hard she was crying. She went to the kitchen sink and squirted a puddle of dishwashing soap into her palm. She returned to the bathroom and scrubbed her baby fine hair for five minutes then rinsed it with the hottest water she could stand. Ma stood up, blotted her hair with a towel, and . . . Ed Grimley lived on.

More snickering. By this time, we were really laughing AT her and WITH her because it was just another joke that had backfired.

Oscar came into the house for some toast before heading to the barn for evening chores. He took one look at his wife with that unicorn-worthy hair horn on her head and just turned around and headed toward the toaster. Nothing fazed him anymore.

Ma dabbed and wiped her hair with paper towels. She blotted with newspapers. Nothing worked. Her hair was as slick as snot on a doorknob.

That night she put a lightweight winter hat on her head and went to bed. The next day she called Kinney's in Massena and asked to speak with the pharmacist. She explained how her young child had smeared Vaseline into her hair and how she'd tried everything to get it out. Kids will be kids, right? She asked what he would recommend.

The pharmacist suggested baby powder or talcum powder to absorb the slick mess. My mother gave her thanks and hung up the phone. It worked. So, there you have it. If you ever put Vaseline into your hair ... um ... I mean if your "child" ever does, just blot it out with some powder.

All kidding aside, children are little sponges. They absorb more than you realize and when they see you doing something, they want to emulate you in the worst way. You're their hero, so they'll do anything to be like you. Most of the time, that's a good thing. When your kids watch you being kind to old people, feeding a stray cat, or picking up a piece of trash and tossing it in the garbage, that's all good stuff. They can also learn from your mistakes if you own up to them and admit that what you did was stupid, dangerous, or harmful to yourself or others.

As I said earlier, my parents deeply regretted smoking. Both of my brothers who picked up that horrible addiction had health issues related to smoking. Tyler was asthmatic since early childhood and becoming addicted to cigarettes definitely did not help his condition. He died from being hit by a drunk driver, so we can't blame the cigarettes for his death. Tim idolized his big brother, and he picked up smoking as a teen. Tim ended up dying from a heart attack at age 53. Other factors were involved, but the cigarette smoking definitely hastened his early demise.

I know people who have unwittingly passed down the smoking/chewing/vaping habit to their children and it saddens me. I think it's because I vividly remember my parents waking up in the morning with that horrible hacking cough. I recall how on edge they were when they tried quitting. The addiction is real and that can be said for anything you put into your body. It doesn't matter if it's nicotine, alcohol, excess food, drugs, whatever. When your little people see you indulging, they automatically believe it's okay for them to consume these things too.

My heart breaks at the memory of my parents expressing their guilt and shame for not being better and doing better. Personally, I think they did fine, all things considered. Still, every parent wants to do right by their kids. Nobody wants to carry the burden of guilt on their shoulders. None of us are perfect. None of us will do everything right. We all make mistakes, whether it's in parenting or just everyday life. Give yourself some grace. Forgive yourself for messing up. Fix what you can. Stop what you should. And remember those kids are sponges. They'll absorb everything you put in front of them, whether it's good or bad. You can't prevent every bad thing from happening to them, but you can certainly change up that "Do as I say, not as I do" rhetoric.

IT'S THE LITTLE THINGS

As I've aged, I find it's the little things that mean the most to me. Grand gestures are fine, but for me it's the smaller, more intimate acts of kindness that put a lump in my throat. With the swelling popularity of Facebook, TikTok, Instagram, and all those other social media outlets, we've become a society of "Look at me!" people. I admit some of those short videos are hilarious. Some are embarrassing. And some just don't make any sense to me at all. Once in a while I'll wonder why a person made a certain video and wonder even more why they posted it for all the world to see. I guess we all want recognition, attention, applause. I'm guilty of it just as much as the next person, but I believe I'm slowing down on that front. At least I hope so.

Lately, it's been the little things that have touched my heart the most. It's the small gestures with the deepest intentions behind them that catch my eye and make me smile. I've been thinking, if I enjoy these sweet gestures, won't other people enjoy them too? I've been trying to incorporate a few more niceties into my life and into those around me who make my life better. I thought I'd share a few of the little things I do that hopefully make a small difference in someone else's life. After all, if we weren't put here to spread kindness, why exist at all? Feel free to steal these ideas. I don't mind.

1. Many years ago before the internet came along, I read a magazine article written by a retired stewardess. You read that

right. Back then these airplane angels were all female and called stewardesses. Today they're flight attendants. This particularly smart lady gave a few tips for a better flight. One of the suggestions she gave was to bring a small bag of candy for the stewardesses. Make sure it's store-bought, unopened, and fresh. Hand it to the first attendant you see and smile. Say good morning and let her know you appreciate her hard work. This will make her day, especially when you know there will always be at least one rowdy and rude passenger on each flight she'll be attending that day. Your $2 investment will let her know she's not just a sky waitress to be ignored or used. You're letting her know she's a valued person in your eyes. I started doing this with every flight I've taken in the past 20 years or so. I do it because I love seeing the surprised faces and smiles on the flight attendants. Whether it's a woman or a man, it makes no difference to me. They're up there in the sky, away from their families for days at a time, dealing with all sorts of people and have no escape. It's not like they can just walk off the job mid-air, right? Once the plane is in flight and drinks or snacks are being served, I'll notice I sometimes receive a few extra packets of cookies, pretzels, or whatever the snack on that flight may be. I must have timed my mini-candy bars gift just right on one trip because the flight attendant came down the aisle, found me, and handed me four small bottles of wine and a clutch of snacks. I just laughed and she said, "You have no idea how today has been. Thank you for the chocolates!" I gave her an appreciative smile and thanked her not only for the snacks, but for all she does. I thought she was going to cry. I don't give those little bags of chocolates expecting extras. That wouldn't be right in my eyes. I just do it because they're doing a job I'd never want, and I appreciate them. Always be nice to your flight attendants.

2. Once in a while I'll bake some cookies and put a few in a baggie and place it in my mailbox with the flag up. My mailman is an excellent cook himself, but when he's working, he's working. This fine young man goes above and beyond to help me when

I'm busy or too damned lazy to go to the post office and mail my own packages. Never has he ever said, "Pendra, I don't have time to mail your packages, so you'll have to make the trip into town yourself." Not once. He's also gone the extra mile to bring my packages right up close to the house so they don't get rained on and ruined. If I can't give him a couple of cookies now and then, that's pretty sad. Of course, he gets a gift card to a local restaurant at Christmastime, but I like to let him know he's appreciated all year long.

3. One great piece of advice I received while traveling came from a member of the housekeeping staff in a Denver hotel. I was lucky enough to catch her as I was heading out for the day, and she was coming in to tidy up my room. I handed her a $20 bill and told her just in case I didn't catch her in the next couple of days, I wanted her to have it. She smiled a big smile and thanked me. She then asked me if there was anything in particular I needed or wanted for my room. I thought about it for a minute and said if she had an extra little bottle of that lovely smelling lotion, that would be great. She nodded and said, "Done!" Then she told me if I ever wanted anything from housekeeping, to just leave a note where they'd find it. I thought that was terribly sweet of her and thanked her for letting me know. That night I went back to my hotel room but didn't find an extra bottle of lotion. Instead, I found a handful of little bottles of that delightful mandarin orange/ginger scented lotion sitting on my bathroom sink. I counted them. Six. Six extra bottles of the most deliciously smelling lotion ever. I laughed. Lesson learned. I felt like a cheapskate, but remembered I was paying $120 per night for the privilege to sleep there, so my guilt dissipated quickly. I'm not a rock star. I don't trash hotel rooms.

A year or so later I was traveling to Tennessee and ended up at the Gaylord Opryland Hotel in Nashville. I remembered that tip about leaving a note for housekeeping, and I'm a sucker for those little trial-size goodies. On my first night I put a $20 bill in the tip envelope and wrote on it "Thank you for doing such a great job. I really enjoy the toiletries." Although I didn't expect anything for giving a tip, the Frugal Freddie in me hoped this would garner me an extra bottle or two of that honeysuckle scented shampoo. I was also curious to see if this was a common courtesy between guest and housekeeper no matter what hotel you're in or what region of the country. I left the next morning, did the tourist thing, and went back to my room in the evening. I'd forgotten about my note until I walked into the bathroom and saw eight rolls of toilet paper stacked on the back of the toilet. Eight rolls. I looked at the sink area and there was only one bottle of shampoo and one bottle of lotion. That's when it hit me. The housekeeper for my floor that day wasn't an English-speaking lady. She must have seen the word "toiletries" and figured maybe I had some digestive issues and needed more toilet tissue! I sat down and roared! She tried. That adorable young lady had done her best to accommodate me and my wishes. I can't imagine having to clean dozens of hotel rooms every day in a bustling city and trying to please everyone. That night I put another $20 in the new envelope and wrote on it "Thank you for the super clean room. I also like the honeysuckle shampoo." The next night I had five little bottles of honeysuckle shampoo on my bathroom sink. When I arrived home, I put one of those shampoo bottles in my shower and giggled the next three times I washed my hair.

4. Not everything has to be about money or gifts. Sometimes it's the gift of time that means the most to people. I've found the gift of sitting and listening to someone for ten minutes can mean the world to some folks. You never know what someone is dealing with, and maybe a chat about the weather is all they need to lighten their load.

Total strangers will brighten and smile if you give them a sincere compliment. Walking out of Walmart last week I noticed a lady in her 40's who appeared to have a lot on her mind. Her expression was one of sadness or maybe just worry. As she approached the store, I looked at her, gave her a big smile, and told her I just loved her fringed skirt. She was wearing a denim skirt with about two inches of neat fringe on the bottom hem of it. It really did look great on her. She lifted her head, looked at me and her smile was brilliant! "Thank you!" was all she said, but her grin told me much more. That five-second exchange cost me nothing but made us both happy.

I guess I'm just turning into a sentimental old fool. All my life I've been so busy working and doing what was necessary to pay my bills, take care of my home, and make my way in this world. Now that I'm retired, I have more time to think of ways to make people around me smile. I love it when someone does something out of the blue for me, so why not return the favor? No grand gestures necessary. Just the little things are fine.

CRAFTY BEAR

"PJ! C'mon, we're going for a ride!" Dennis (we all called him Denny) had wheeled his battered old blue Ford pickup truck into my driveway that Saturday morning just as I was about to mow my lawn. "The lawn can wait. I'm on a mission. Hop in."

This was in the summer of 1991, and I was on my long weekend off and had plenty of time to mow later. I hopped up into Denny's cowboy Cadillac and off we went. "Where are we headed?" I asked.

"Up to Lake Placid. I've been in touch with a lady who has an antique dresser that I think I want. She advertised it in the newspaper, and it sounds exactly like what I've been looking for to finish up my master bedroom." Denny had just built a new log cabin home and was taking his time furnishing it. He didn't want to throw just anything into his new place, so he hand-picked each and every item that crossed the threshold. "If it's what I think it is, she's practically giving it away. It's huge, but if we take the drawers out and the mirror off, I'm pretty sure you'll be able to help me move it." He cast an appreciative glance at me then pretending to talk to himself he quietly said, "Always make friends with strong farm kids."

I rolled my eyes and said, "Oh, so this is all about USING me?" His infectious grin spread across his fifty-five-year-old face. He was old enough to be my father, yet never treated me like a child. He respected me as an adult but would still offer a bit of advice now and then . . . but always as a friend. He was never condescending or patronizing.

Denny took his time driving through the foothills of the

Adirondacks, following notes on a piece of yellow paper torn from a legal pad. I glanced at his chicken scratching and could barely make out directions and landmarks. We chatted about what was going on in our lives, work, families, and anything that popped into our heads. He pawed through his cassette case and snapped a T. Graham Brown tape into the player. I smiled. Before long we were both belting out, "Got a letter this mornin' from my first ex-wife . . . there ain't enough money to get her outta my life . . ." We always laughed when we heard that song because he'd been married twice, and these lyrics hit so close to home for him. After almost two hours of conversation and music, Denny pointed out a wooden bear standing about three feet high. He was at the end of a driveway and was holding a small board with a number on it. "Here we are!" he said excitedly as we finally pulled into the long gravel drive. After driving a couple of slow minutes, the woods opened and we saw it.

The "camp" that held this coveted antique dresser turned out to be a three-story home built in the typical Adirondack style. Plenty of timber and glass. Most of the windows looked out over a small lake. I gave Denny a bug-eyed stare, raised my eyebrows and let out a slow whistle. "Whew! If this is a camp, I'd love to see their home!" I was pretty sure my whole house would have fit into one of the bedrooms in this joint.

Denny put the truck in park and flipped the key. Total silence except for the sound of the loons on the water. Oh yeah. This is doable. I could get lazy here for sure. I followed as Denny headed toward the main entrance. He gave the doorbell button a tickle and we heard a faint ting-a-ling inside. After a few seconds, a short, stocky woman about sixty years old came to the door. She was all smiles and reminded me of an overfed puppy looking for another treat. "HELLO! You must be Denny here to pick up the dresser!" She reached out and pumped his right hand enthusiastically. "I'm so glad you made it because I really want to get rid of it. It's just too big and we bought a new bedroom set and this just does NOT fit our style anymore!" Holy cow, woman, I thought. Take a breath. Her gray hair was twisted up into tight curls on her bobbing head. Her dangling earrings whipped to the front and back of her jawline every time she nodded or swiveled her head. I think they call these people animated conversationalists.

"I'm just here to look at it, Jenny. I hope it's what I want, but we'll see." Denny explained it wasn't a done deal yet. Not a sight unseen kind of exchange. He introduced me and she eagerly tried to wrench my arm out of its socket. I could tell she was thinking if Denny didn't want this behemoth of a dresser, maybe I'd take it off her hands. We walked through the foyer and her husband came into view. We all stood in one of the most glorious kitchens I'd ever seen. Jenny introduced us to her husband Phil. Phil noticed my childlike awe of their kitchen and looked over at his wife.

"Why don't you take Denny to see the furniture and I'll show this young lady around down here?" Jenny nodded and nearly yanked poor Denny off his feet as she hauled him toward the staircase. Phil turned around and said to me, "I hope you're not in any hurry. Jenny's got a lot more than one dresser up there for him to look at." Then he let out a sigh and said, "That poor guy." I told Phil I was just along for the ride and for a little extra muscle if necessary. He then proceeded to give me a tour of his kitchen. I was green with envy at all the counter space, the shiny appliances, their built-in pantry, the EXTRA pantry just off the kitchen which held every small appliance imaginable.

I looked at Phil and asked, "Did I die? Is this Heaven?"

He gave a hearty laugh and said, "You ain't seen nothin' yet!" then led me to the great room. Rough-hewn beams crisscrossed above my head. The wall facing the lake consisted of magnificent windows from floor to ceiling, with the ones at the top cut into triangular shapes. Heavy wooden furniture covered in browns and dark greens anchored the room nicely. Red pillows adorned the sofas and chairs. I felt as if I'd just stepped into a fancy hotel. As Phil told me about how the house was built, I stood there soaking up all its glorious beauty. I was just a country bumpkin raised on a small farm. Wealth like this was so new to me. This was a scene from the movies. Phil could see I was loving it and made me feel right at home. He invited me to sit because, as he put it, "Once Jenny gets you in her grips, you're not getting out anytime soon." He nodded toward the upstairs and jokingly muttered, "That poor bastard."

That's when I noticed an enormous bearskin rug in front of their larger fireplace. (There was a smaller fireplace at the other end of the great room.) "WOW! Is that real?" My innocence was showing, but I didn't care. I had no experience with rich people. I didn't know if they bought real pelts or just fake ones that didn't stink or shed.

Phil followed my eyes and started smiling.

"Yes, that's real. And there's a bit of a story behind it. Make yourself comfy and I'll tell you how that bear came to be a permanent fixture here." He kicked his feet up on a plush recliner.

"We had this place built almost twenty-two years ago. Back then this area hadn't been developed much. We have a bit of acreage, so it took a lot of time and money to clear enough just to get a road back into this spot. Then clearing an area for the house was another daunting task. In case you hadn't noticed, this is a big house." He winked at me. His sarcasm wasn't lost on me, and he loved that. "Jenny and I used to come up here all the time during construction. We had a little tow-behind camper that we left off to one side, out of the way. After the first couple of weekends here, we scabbed on a couple of rooms so we wouldn't feel so claustrophobic. We'd drive up, rough it for a few days, check out the progress the contractors were making, then head back home. Well, one time we pulled in here and our little camp was torn up. We thought it was just some vandals at first, damned kids with nothing to do but wreck other peoples' property. Then we got looking and we saw it wasn't kids. It was animals. And by the looks of the tracks, it was probably bears. Well, we cleaned up the camp as best we could. We repaired everything we needed and threw out what was beyond fixing. A few weeks later, the same thing happened. Our camp was violated. That's the only word I can use. I got pissed and started walking the woods with my gun. I was going to get that son of a bitch, but no such luck. We locked everything up, took all the food out, and went back home. The next weekend I had a plan. I borrowed my friend's truck with a camper on it and drove that up here. Jenny was busy so she didn't come with me that weekend. I was going to nail this monster come hell or high water. I didn't care if it was hunting season or not, this guy was going DOWN!" Phil looked over at the rug and pulled an imaginary trigger with his right index finger.

"Don't tell me, let me guess." I had it all figured out. Or so I thought. "You waited in your friend's camper and when the bear came back, you blasted him."

"Not even close." Phil kicked back in his recliner a few more inches. His chin jutted toward the bear and said, "I outsmarted him. On my way up here, I stopped at a bakery and bought a dozen jelly filled doughnuts. I also swiped a bottle of my wife's sleeping pills. She hasn't taken them in ages. She says they make her too groggy the next day, but she never bothered to throw them out. I also brought four jars of that god-awful glitter she used for her crafting projects. Back then all the ladies were in to making those gaudy crafts that looked like a drunken kindergarten kid threw together. But don't tell her I said that."

At that moment I was getting concerned for this man. He was definitely older, but not ancient. He didn't seem to be crazy or mentally irregular in any way. His wife was still upstairs with Denny looking at all of the furniture. I couldn't look to anyone else for an explanation for doughnuts and glitter, so I just sat there waiting for him to explain.

"Ah, I see that look of confusion in your eyes." Phil was nodding and waving a hand at me as if he'd just read my mind about his mental stability. "So, here's the scoop: I'm not really much of a hunter. And I can find my way around this property pretty well now but back then before much was cleared, I could get lost easily. I knew if I went hunting the outcome might not be so good. I baited that bear with the doughnuts. I put the sleeping pills in the doughnuts. I mean, I really loaded those suckers up. I didn't know if I had enough to kill him, which is what I was hoping so I wouldn't really have to pull the trigger myself, or if it was even enough to make him sleepy. I put the laced doughnuts over near that big maple tree." He pointed out toward the right side of the house. "I dumped the glitter in a circle around the doughnuts. I made sure to use the really bright stuff and put it in a big ring around the piled-up pastries."

Okay, this guy was really off his rocker. I stole a nervous glance at the staircase hoping to see Denny. I could hear his voice wafting down but no movement. I was stuck with this jelly doughnut and glitter-crazed man.

"I parked the camper and I watched. I waited. Nothing. I stayed up until 2:30 a.m. Finally, I couldn't keep my eyes open any longer and I dozed off. I only slept about four hours then woke up, went outside, and sure enough the damned doughnuts were gone. I grabbed my gun and flashlight. It was light out, but I knew the flashlight would reflect off the glitter in the shadows of the trees."

AHA, I thought. Maybe this guy isn't crazy. I'd never heard of using glitter to track an animal. Then again, I'd never heard of slipping a few sleeping pills into doughnuts before, so . . . yeah. Who am I to judge?

"I followed his tracks. Now and then they'd intersect with other tracks, but when I put the flashlight on them, the glitter showed up each time. I don't know if you've ever done crafts, or if you're around little kids much, but you can NOT get that shit off. Glitter is FOREVER. Instead of ink bombs on money packs, they should just put glitter bombs in them. You'd be able to spot a bank robber a mile off." Phil stared off into space for a few seconds as he thought about that genius solution.

"So, you're telling me you tracked THAT bear by the glitter on his paws?" I was still 50/50 on his story. I'm gullible. I was worse back then.

"Yes, ma'am, I did. As God is my witness, I tracked that beast with a flashlight. I finally found him sprawled out between two big rocks. They're still on the right-hand side of the driveway as you go out, right after that big curve, about twenty feet from the edge of the driveway. It looked like he was making his way between them and decided to take a nap." He put his two fists out in front of his face, side by side to demonstrate how the rocks were sitting.

"And . . . was he dead? Did you overdose the bear?" I was almost buying it. In all honesty, I wanted to buy his story because it was just too off the wall.

"He wasn't dead. He was just sleeping. Snoring, as a matter of fact. He still had a little bit of powder and jelly from the doughnuts on the side of his face. That made me laugh a little bit, but I didn't waste any time. I had no idea exactly when he'd eaten the doughnuts or how long he'd be out. I put my gun right behind his front leg and pulled the trigger. I made sure I aimed it so I'd hit his heart but not the rock behind him. There was a grunt, then some wheezing, then . . . nothing. I didn't really feel like much of a hunter that day. Actually, I felt pretty shitty about it. Then I thought about how he'd ruined our camp and how he'd ruin us if he ever felt like attacking us on a whim. I already knew he was comfortable coming to our building site. It was only a matter of time before we'd run into him and be at his mercy."

I nodded and agreed with him. I didn't hunt at that time, but I came from a hunting family and understood what he meant. There are some chances you can take, others you can't. Nor should you. I told Phil I thought he did the right thing. It was his land and he had a right to protect himself and his wife.

"I gutted him out right there. It took me a bit of time to drag the body back, but I did it. I got him rolled into a tarp and loaded into the camper. Man, do bears stink. My buddy knew a guy who did taxidermy and took care of the rest for me, no questions asked. Funny how a little extra cash helps things move along. And that's how Glitter became a permanent fixture here."

"Glitter? You named your bear . . . GLITTER? Sounds like a stripper's name!" I giggled.

"Well, c'mon! What else COULD I call him?"

Just then we heard footsteps on the stairs and saw Jenny and Denny (how cute does that sound) come down. "You would not believe all the antiques they have up there." Denny looked like a kid who had just stepped into a candy store for the first time ever. Phil looked at me with an "I told you so" look.

Denny and Jenny had struck a deal on several pieces of antique furniture. Denny decided he'd hire a moving company to come with a van to grab everything in one fell swoop. Jenny's prices were more than fair, and she was tickled to get rid of the furniture she didn't want any longer. Denny felt like he'd just won the lottery. A win-win all around.

We all said our good-byes and Denny and I headed for his truck. We got in and just after we rounded the wide bend in the driveway, I looked off to my right and at about twenty feet in I saw two large rocks, side by side. I smiled as we rode past them and looked over at Denny. "Wanna hear a cool story?" I asked.

WHERE THERE'S
A WILL...

Way back in 1976, Oscar received word from one of his siblings that their elderly aunt was about to go belly up and join her husband in the afterlife. Aunt Rose and Uncle George never had any children of their own, so when Uncle George died, everything went to his wife, Rose. Aunt Rose was quite fond of her ten nieces and nephews and had updated her will to split a sizable sum of money in her bank account among the ten children. I say children, but by that time my father and his siblings were well into their late 30's with some pushing 50. Everyone in the family knew of Aunt Rose's wishes and appreciated her extreme generosity.

The day finally came when Aunt Rose passed. All the relatives were contacted, arrangements were made, and my father donned his black suit for the fourth time in two years. That's what happens when all the aunts and uncles start dropping, sort of like a domino effect. Then, something odd happened. Aunt Rose's will couldn't be found. They searched her home but found nothing. In New York state, if a person dies intestate (no will), the closest family member gets the loot. (After probate, of course. The state has to get its piece of the pie.) Well, now, wouldn't you know, Rose's sister Edith was the closest living relative; therefore, she would inherit that sizable bank account intended for the nieces and nephews. Edith wasn't hurting financially, but she was never one to turn down a penny or two.

My father and his siblings weren't vultures by any means, but they all KNEW Aunt Rose had specifically named the ten of them in her will. This gnawed at my father. A few days went by and Oscar devised a plan. Remember, back then there wasn't any caller I.D. on the phones. Oscar decided to call his Aunt Edith. This is how the exchange went that fateful day in 1976:

"Hello, this is John Mulrooney from the law office of Hyde, Beach, and Mulrooney in Albany New York. May I please speak with Edith, a surviving sibling of Mrs. George King also known as Rose?" His voice sounded SO professional!

"Yes, this is her. I'm Rose's sister Edith. What's this all about?"

"Well, ma'am, we understand Rose King has passed and we're trying to settle her estate," Mr. "Mulrooney said. "Have you located her will yet?"

"Oh dear. I've searched my sister's house top to bottom and just could NOT find her will. I'm sorry, but it's just nowhere to be found!"

Riiiiight, Aunt Edith. I'll bet you knew EXACTLY where to look for it. That's what my father was thinking that whole time.

"Ma'am, we have here in our home office a will that was drawn up for your sister several years ago naming you as sole beneficiary of her entire estate. This includes her bank accounts, real estate, vehicles, and any other assets she may have had at the time of her demise. BUT . . . we can't execute this will unless we have the original will that was written prior to this one. We need to confirm the dates and make sure we're executing the latest will and granting Rose King's last wishes. Is there ANY way you could possibly take another look in the house, or maybe a safe deposit box to find the original will? It must be voided before we can continue with the legal proceedings. If not, this may take years to go through and everything will be on hold until all legal avenues are completed. You will eventually get what's left in the accounts minus our fees and any funds the state withholds. You can't legally sell her real estate or personal property until everything is settled and in your name. But if we had that original will, that would validate this newer will completely and everything should go quickly and smoothly."

Oscar could hear his Aunt Edith salivating at the thought of inheriting EVERYTHING.

"Mr. Mulrooney, give me another couple of days to look again. Maybe she had a drawer I didn't check. I'll go through every inch of Rose's home again."

"Thank you very much! Today's Friday, so if you happen to find Rose's old will, would you please drop it off at our associate's office in Malone? They're doing the legwork on the local paperwork for this estate, and it would save some time instead of mailing it to us down here in Albany." Oscar then gave his Aunt Edith the name and address of the attorney in Malone who was actually handling Aunt Rose's estate.

"Oh, absolutely! Anything I can do to help get this over with as quickly as possible." Aunt Edith was almost gleeful.

Fewer than three days later, Oscar received a call from Uncle George's and Aunt Rose's attorney in Malone. Seems like Aunt Edith DID find that original will after all. Imagine her surprise when she handed it over to the lawyer and asked about the "other" will. The Malone attorney had NO idea what she was talking about and shook his head. Aunt Edith told him about the telephone conversation with Mr. Mulrooney from their head office in Albany. Again, the attorney shook his head and told her they weren't part of a big law firm. They were just a simple two-man shop. Just two guys from Malone who stayed in Malone. He thanked her for finding the will and promised to execute it as soon as possible.

A few weeks later, Oscar and each of his siblings received checks for about $4,000. It doesn't sound like a lot of money by today's standards, but back then when Oscar was just trying to get his feet under him on a farm, $4,000 was like winning the lottery.

Oscar didn't immediately tell his brothers and sisters about the phone call Aunt Edith had received from the Albany attorney. Eventually Aunt Edith passed (and, yes, Oscar was a pallbearer), and only then did word leak out about Oscar helping Aunt Rose rest in peace. Her last wishes had been carried out the way she had wanted. So, the next time you hear someone say, "Aw, he's just a dumb farmer," you might want to bite your tongue.

MICK'S BOOKS

My mother was wise beyond her years. When I think of the brilliant ideas she had when my siblings and I were young, I'm in awe. Her creativity was endless when it came to child rearing. She made mistakes like any parent, but she always owned up to them and fixed what she could. She was strict, but not mean. Loving, yet not overbearing. We were encouraged to communicate and express our feelings. We had rules to follow, but even as a kid I found they were reasonable. I do remember there was one thing that wasn't allowed to be said in our home. Marilyn C. King would not tolerate any of us kids saying we were bored. I still can't utter the phrase "I'm bored" because of her simple statement when I was a child: only lazy and ignorant people can be bored.

Wow. That hit hard! Was my own mother calling me lazy and ignorant? No. She would go on to explain her reasoning. If you had an ample imagination, you could never be bored. If you were smart, you would find ways to amuse yourself, whether it was to read a book, write a story, or go on an adventure outside. We were pushed to explore our little corner of the world. We had plenty of places to build forts, clubhouses, or spy headquarters. There was always plenty of paper and pens to scribble down our thoughts or plans. Books were in every room of the house, so there was no shortage of learning material. Our dining room had one wall that was nothing but books, floor to ceiling, corner to doorway. My brother-from-another-mother Jeff is fond of telling me about one of his first memories of stepping into our house. He recalls that huge built-in bookcase and the multitude of books it held; it mesmerized him.

He wasn't the only visitor who was astonished at not only the number of books, but the variety of topics they contained. A large portion of the tomes consisted of subjects such as life after death, ESP, reincarnation, religions, and spirituality. My mother was fascinated by the possibility of our spirits living on and sending messages to those still in their fleshy containers. Most of her books were written by recognized experts on the topics of the afterlife and the unexplained. Many volumes were penned by people with real experiences. Mick always loved the books that were written by doubters who had experienced events that were beyond explanation. She used to hand a book over to me and say, "Here's another one of those naysayers who is now a believer." Those stories always tickled her because they validated her own spooky moments. My mother was a lifelong student with a multitude of interests. If she'd lived long enough, I'm sure she'd have appreciated the ease and speed of the internet, but her loyalty would have always been with books.

Mick's books held magic. Not black magic, but the magic of learning. There were books on self-improvement. Books on home improvement. The thick ones were usually reference books on either health, gardening, or the arts. We had the 1970's staple *Encyclopedia Britannica*. I remember thumbing through a hefty volume of the World Wars. Most of the pictures were in black and white, which to me made them even more scary than if they were in full color. Reading about wars never made sense to me as a child and even less sense as an adult. Back to the magic books. They held stories of faraway lands and their people. Different cultures, lifestyles, foods, and money were shared on so many pages. With the flip of a finger, I could be in another country. I might be on another continent. Maybe I'd be surrounded by penguins or tribes of jungle inhabitants. The possibilities were endless.

My mother knew the true value of books. Whether it was a book she paid a dime for at a garage sale, or one she special-ordered through the mail, she treasured each and every book she owned. Some were dog-eared and well loved. Others were read, but only once. She told us it was a privilege to have books and a gift to learn to read. And she was right. Looking back on it now, I think my love of travel came from reading about faraway places. It's not that I wasn't happy at home, I just knew there was a huge world out there that needed to be explored. As the years piled up on me, I found myself in several places I'd only read about, and it was exhilarating. Seeing the Colosseum in person is much different than seeing a picture of it in a book. Visiting the Eagle's Nest in Germany where Hitler held meetings was unnerving yet educational. Watching real kangaroos hopping freely in Australia was surreal.

Every now and then I'll run into someone who tells me they hate reading. I can't comprehend this. Maybe they were forced to read dry or uninteresting material when they were young. How sad. I remember having to read dreadful books in school. They didn't hold my attention, but I had to slog through them if I wanted to write that book report or get an A in the class. Required reading was sometimes painful, so I can see where this would scar a child and put them off books forever. I'm so grateful my mother had a buffet of books available to us for our evolving little brains. She knew we needed a plethora of topics to keep us interested in reading, so she supplied just that. Whether it was books or magazines like *Reader's Digest* and *National Geographic*, we always had something interesting to feast our eyes upon. Of all the gifts you can give a child, what greater gift can you give than the ability to read? Fostering the love of the written word is something that can never be taken away or lost. It carries on with us throughout our lifetime and it can be a great comfort in times of loss or sadness. Reading can lift your spirits when you're down. Reading can fill lonely hours and take your heart and mind to a better place. Reading can make you understand another's point of view and broaden your horizons. You don't always have to agree with the author, but you can take a few minutes to learn why they feel the way they do. Sometimes we learn about ourselves through books. There are ways to improve our lives and the lives of those around us through books. A cure-all? Maybe not, but books sure can't hurt.

Like my mother, I read books on numerous topics. I soak up the knowledge the author is imparting, especially if it's something I can use in my own life. It tickles me to learn about a new subject from someone who is willing to share their insight and experience. I encourage others to write books and publish them because you never know who will gain something from what you have to offer. And yes, you ARE a writer if you write. Whether you self-publish or go to an established publishing house, you are a writer. You are an author. Write those books. Spread the wealth of your knowledge and experience. Ignore those jealous and ignorant, petty naysayers who say you can't or shouldn't. Do it for yourself. The satisfaction of writing is just as grand as reading.

Long before the Internet, Google, and YouTube, we had books. I admit it's easier and faster to type in a question or phrase and come up with an answer in 2.2 seconds than to paw through a book. How thrilling to have that much knowledge and power at your fingertips! Literally. I love the ease and convenience of my computer and cell phone. As I age, I like things easier. And yet . . . sometimes I like going old school. Once in a while I like holding a thick reference book in my hand and flipping through the pages until I find what I want or need. There's something satisfying about holding an actual book in my hands that still thrills me. It's not quite the same with my Kindle. I've had the same Kindle for 15 years. Maybe longer. I don't use it much but, when I do, I appreciate the convenience. I particularly appreciate the compact size and how it will hold all the books I want in its small body. It is the perfect appliance for travel, and I've counted on it many times as I've held an airline ticket in one hand and my Kindle in the other. Once I get back home it's a different story. I want my books. I want to immerse myself in the feel and smell of a real book. Some people laugh at me for this, while others nod their heads knowingly.

Mick's books were magic, no doubt about it. After she died

in 2002, we did as she had requested and cleaned her belongings out of the house. I took a handful of her tattered volumes because I knew they were the ones she loved the most. I have them on my bookshelf and once in a while I'll pick up her dream analysis book to decipher a dream. Or maybe I'll read about astral projection. Perhaps I'll peruse a chapter or two about paranormal activity. These books are all interesting, but they also give me a sense of comfort. As I thumb through the pages, I can almost feel my mother's hand guiding me. And if that's not magic, I don't know what is.

TIDBITS

You know I love old people and could sit and listen to them for hours. Hell, I HAVE listened to them for hours and I'm grateful for those times. Some of those conversations were hilarious, filled with funny stories from the past. Other visits were more somber and serious. Then there were the ones that turned out to be helpful. A few were entertaining and I'd walk away wondering if my leg had just been pulled. Chances are, my legs were yanked more times than I'd care to admit. I never begrudged an older friend pulling one over on me. I enjoyed a good joke or stunt as well as the next person, so I didn't mind if they polished my Miss Gullible crown from time to time.

While visually strolling through my notebooks, I found more tidbits of good advice, superstitions, habits, and general observations on life. I must have thought they'd come in handy, and that's why I wrote them down so many years ago. Looking at the list now, I'm smiling because I actually do follow some of the advice or use the information in my own life. Funny how everything comes back to us, huh? In no particular order, here are a few more gems gleaned from my collections.

1. Never dehorn a young heifer or bull unless the month you're doing it has an "r" in it. This was one of Oscar's beliefs and it made sense. You never wanted to take the big horn snippers to the animal's head during the hot months of May, June, July, or August because the critters tend to bleed more when it's warm outside. If you dehorned your cattle in the cooler months, the blood would clot more quickly and that's better for the animal.

2. "One potato, two potato, three potato, four" was what ol' Ernie was taught by his mom when he was young. She knew drinking water was a good idea when you first woke up, so she taught Ernie to drink "four taters' worth of water" every morning. He'd fill the glass and start gulping. One potato (gulp), two potato (gulp) . . . Every now and then when I'm taking a few swigs of water I'll catch myself thinking one potato, two potato . . . and then I laugh.

3. Margaret gave me this tidbit she learned from her grandmother. "You know how it is when you're just a young kid. You believe everything your parents tell you. My mom used to tell us we had to floss our teeth every night, otherwise we'd have nightmares. We'd all had nightmares before, so we knew how awful they were. We were so diligent about flossing. It wasn't until years later we realized our mother was a dental hygienist and was just doing her job at home as well as at the office."

4. Roger had a good one for getting his kids to take care of their clothes from their laundry baskets. When Roger and his wife would do laundry, they'd put each child's clothing in their own color-coded basket. The kids were to fold their clothes and put everything away in dressers or hang the items in their closets. Once their clothes were put away, they'd use the empty baskets and a few blankets to build a fort in one of the bedrooms. Roger or his wife would then read stories from their favorite books to them. With four little kids to wrangle, this worked like a charm. The older two kids would help the younger two, so they'd all get to build the fort sooner. To this day, all four of their children love to read and now they build story forts with their own offspring.

5. I know a gentleman who is an avid hunter. He's in his 70's now, but still gets out there every fall for deer season. Whenever he gets his big buck, he takes a few drops of blood from the deer and places it on his skin over his heart. He said he was taught to do this as a way to honor the deer and to thank him for feeding

his family. He also said it was good luck and would help him bag another buck the following year. I want to laugh at this one, but he has pictures and old tags dating back many years. He hasn't been skunked since 1969.

6. Clutter seems to be a big problem in this day and age of consumerism. Most of us get caught up in the trap of "needing" the latest gizmo or fashion. I know this older couple whose home is always very comfortable, yet never cluttered. It's not stark by any means, but it's definitely in the minimalist style. One day I asked how they keep everything so organized and eye pleasing. They told me they have a "One in, two out" policy now. Whenever they bring one thing into the house, whether it's an item of clothing or a new pan, they'll find two items to donate or throw away. As long as they get two things out, they're happy. They started doing this about ten years ago and said they should have started much sooner. They don't miss a thing they've given away and their lives are much happier with fewer objects taking up space. I've been pretty good about the "One in, one out" method, but I need to step it up. I'll be trying the "One in, two out" idea to see if that helps me declutter my home.

7. A fireman friend of mine has two kids. He and his wife let their kids "feed" the smoke detectors in their rooms every year on their birthdays. They let the children take the old battery out of the smoke detector and then put the new one in and test it. They want it to be second nature for their kids to have working, dependable smoke detectors throughout their lives. Performing this birthday ritual is one way they hope to instill a good habit in them. Dave said he never wants to see another burn victim in his lifetime. I don't blame him.

8. I knew an elderly lady who always kept the bones from any meat she cooked. She'd put them in a big plastic bag and place them in the freezer. About once a month she'd make a delicious broth from all of these bones. One day I was at her house and as she took the bones out of her big kettle of simmering water on

the stove, I reached for them. I was going to throw them out for her, but she quickly stopped me. "No! Never throw the bones in the garbage! Toss them on the woodpile out back." I did as she had instructed, figuring she was giving the used bones to the wildlife in her backyard. I was wrong. Whenever she'd have a fire outside or in her wood stove inside, she'd burn some bones. She went on to tell me about the old rituals of "bone fires" which eventually became bonfires. There are several concepts of bone fires, including the one about Guy Fawkes, but my friend said she didn't care about that history. She believed in burning bones as a way to ward off evil spirits. I laughed and told her I never felt anything evil at her house. She gave me a coy smile and said, "See? It works."

9. Helen told me she always makes the right decision between two choices when she rubs her right eyebrow. I really chuckled at this one. She told me to try it. "Next time you're really in a quandary about something, take your finger and lightly stroke your right eyebrow from the bridge of your nose to the outer edge. Do that slowly for a minute or two, and you'll come up with an answer. I've never regretted my right eyebrow decisions." I've never really kept score, but maybe it's just that extra minute of consideration that gives me better decisiveness. I might have to pay attention to this for the next month or so just to see if it makes a difference. If not, no harm done.

10. An acquaintance of mine puts a small glass of wine out on her lawn on the eleventh of every month. I asked her if it was to attract and kill bugs, or maybe to repel little varmints, or possibly for the bees? I had no idea. She laughed at me and shook her head. No. No. No. None of those reasons. When I asked why she did that, all she said was that her mother and grandmother used to do it, and there are some things she just can't share with me. I never did find out what a glass of wine on the 11th of every month meant. Maybe it was a family thing. Or maybe she was into some kind of hoodoo voodoo juju to which I am totally

oblivious. I'm tempted to start putting a glass of wine outside every month just to see if anything out of the ordinary happens to me. I'll keep you posted.

11. Shelly can't have any more than three lamps in her living room. She'd been given a nice floor lamp for Christmas one year, so she put it up immediately and then took another lamp out of the living room. Her son commented on how the room could really use more light, so why not leave that lamp in there? The look on her face was priceless. She was utterly shocked. Shelly explained that it's bad luck to have more than three lamps in any room. When pressed for more information about how and where that started, she said she didn't know any of the particulars. All she knew was it was bad luck to have too many lamps. If I had to guess, I'd say her folks or grandparents were miserly and didn't want to buy more light bulbs or have a higher electric bill from too many lights being left on. Or maybe there IS something about the number four for lamps? If anyone reading this has four lamps in any room, please take one out for a couple of weeks and let me know what happens.

12. I worked with an older gentleman who shared a story about going to a friend's house for dinner. Hugh remembered sitting down at the big dining room table with his friend Arnold. Arnold's mom put bowls and platters of food on the table. Everyone helped themselves and chatted while enjoying their meal. The mom reminded them there was pie for dessert, to make sure they left room in their bellies. When it was time for dessert, Arnold and all of his siblings flipped their empty plates over and placed them upside down on the table. Mom then dished out a piece of pie for every plate that was flipped. Hugh had never seen this before, and his face must have shown his bewilderment. The dad then explained, "Hugh, we let our kids eat as much as they want because they work hard on the farm. What we don't stand for is wasting anything, especially food. We taught the kids early on they can take as much as they want

for dinner, but they have to eat what they take. You can only have dessert if you can flip your empty plate over to the clean side." Hugh thought about it for a minute then smiled. He'd eaten all he'd taken and man, that pie looked great! He quickly flipped his dinner plate upside down and was happily served a piece of warm pie.

Everyone has stories to tell, habits ingrained in them, or superstitions they follow. Hearing about other people and the way they think, the things they believe, and the rituals they adhere to has always interested me. I only wish I could follow some of these thoughts back to their origins. I'm sure the original stories made sense at the time, or possibly made no sense at all! I strongly encourage you to chat up an older person or two and get some of these tales out of them. If they happen to be family members, that's even better. Why not pass down some family traditions or possibly pick up a few new ones? Might be fun.

A LETTER TO FIRENZE

I was excited as I drove my truck 12 miles to pick you up that bright spring morning. Plans were made, supplies were bought, and I was ready. More than ready. I wanted you from the first moment I laid eyes on your picture. You were one of eight, but you seemed to stick out from the rest. I knew you were mine. I felt it in my heart as soon as I looked into your big, brown eyes.

I pulled into the dusty driveway and put it in park. When my feet hit the ground, I had the urge to run to the garage where you were, but I didn't. I tried to act cool and collected. And I did . . . until I entered and heard you and your siblings yipping away in happiness. "Today's the day," I thought. All eight of you will be going to new homes where you'll be loved, cherished, and spoiled. YOU, more than any of the rest, I'm sure. I'll teach you to go outside when you need to relieve yourself. I'll show you how to behave properly when company comes to visit. We'll be buddies and constant companions. We'll have great adventures and do everything together.

And we did.

I named you Firenze, the Italian version of Florence. I'd been to that beautiful city in Italy and fell in love with her grace and beauty. I figured the name fit. I called you "Renzi" for short because really, who doesn't have a nickname? And I really couldn't bring myself to call you Florence. You were not a geriatric housewife.

At first, I laughed at your crazy puppy antics. Your feet were too big for your body. You clomped around the house as if you were wearing clown shoes. Your little needle teeth were sharp, but you never meant to pierce my skin, it just accidentally happened now and then when we were playing. I'd never get mad at you for that. Your hair was so fine and soft when you were a baby. Cuddling you was like holding a stuffed toy from the store, only better because I'd always get plenty of loving back.

You followed me everywhere: to the kitchen for a cup of coffee, and to my recliner when I was watching the news. We'd walk to the bathroom where you'd stand guard as I laughed about it. You made sure I wasn't drowning every time I took a bath or shower. Hell, several times you hopped into the shower with me because it looked like I was having way too much fun by myself!

Mealtime was never an issue. You'd eat whatever I put in front of you and happily look up at me every time I filled your bowl, even if it was the same ol' kibble you'd eaten yesterday. And the day before. Rarely could I ever say no when you'd give me that look as I was eating. I'd say 99.999% of the time part of my breakfast, lunch, or supper would end up in my fingertips and held in front of you. You must have had a cast iron stomach right from the get-go because you'd eat anything proffered. Sometimes you'd make me laugh with your wrinkled up nose or your stuck tongue. You always appreciated every nibble, and I could see that in your eyes.

Oh, the adventures we had! All of the hiking we did in the woods. Up and down so many mountains. Swimming in rivers and lakes. Snowshoeing was always a blast as you pounced on every square inch of untouched snow you could find. I'd roar every time you made like a plow and pushed your face through the drifts. I'd shake my head as you dug deep and all I could see was your hind end and wagging tail. We visited friends and relatives, and you were welcomed with open arms everywhere. Your good manners paid off in dividends such as extra biscuits or tidbits from dinner plates. Threats of being dognapped were common, but never taken too seriously.

You were more than my pet. You were my friend,

confidant, and companion. You were my sounding board when I was in a fix. You never judged or snubbed me like people do. Your unconditional love was more than I could have ever hoped for in this life. Every time you looked at me, I saw nothing but pure adoration and acceptance. You never asked for explanations or reasons. You just took me as I was, warts and all. Oh, how I loved you for that!

Even in my deepest, darkest moments, you never left me. You kept me on track and kept me going when I didn't think I could continue. There were days when I couldn't drag myself out of bed, but you walked into the bedroom and quietly placed your chin next to my pillow, your liquid brown eyes staring into mine. You were talking to me, telling me I'd be fine. And you were right. I'd crawl out of bed and head outside with you for a little while. Then we'd take a walk. When we returned home, I'd always feel so much better. Are you sure you weren't a doctor? Maybe that should be spelled dogtor? You healed me and you healed my heart repeatedly. You were with me through good times and bad and I can't say thank you enough.

One day I noticed your face was getting a little whiter. A few light hairs started sprouting on your muzzle and forehead. Before long, you had more white than brown on your head. I laughed, as I was doing the same. I had more white than when we first met. Funny how we did everything together, including getting older. Our walks became a little shorter. Our hikes weren't as steep as before. Our jaunts in the snow took more time than previously, but we did them. Time started slowing down for both of us, but I could see it in you more than in myself.

Then the inevitable happened. Your eyesight was diminished to only shadows. Your teeth had either fallen out or were too soft to eat much food. You apologized for every accident inside the house, even though you couldn't help it. Getting up and walking was just too painful, and you were suffering. Every single day I prayed for you to have a good day, for you to rally and find the strength to go on. I selfishly wished for more time than what I was allowed, and I felt guilty. Every moment with you was a blessing and I wasn't ready to give you up. And yet . . . I knew I had to. I knew I loved you enough to not let you suffer for my own selfish reasons. You looked me in the eye and told me it was time.

I cradled you in my arms and held you while the tears poured from my eyes. I could feel my heart squeezing in my chest, knowing I'd never love like this again. Finally, after what seemed like only a minute but was much longer, I stood up, carried you outside, and placed you in the back seat. I cried all the way to the vet's office. I second-guessed myself at least a dozen times, but in my heart and soul, I knew I was doing right by you. As I carried you inside, I noticed other people were in the waiting room. They glanced up and saw the pain on my face. They nodded with that knowing, sympathetic look that only animal lovers can convey. We went directly to the back room where the assistant helped me place you on a table with a soft blanket. She made sure you were as comfortable as possible. The doctor came in and shook my hand. He carefully and lovingly checked you over and then gave me that look. No words were necessary. He and his assistant politely turned their backs to me and busied themselves at the counter for a moment. I know it didn't take that long to fill the syringe, but they were kind enough to not hurry my good-bye with you. I sat on a stool next to you with my arms wrapped around your body. I thought I was all cried out, but I was wrong. More tears flowed and they fell on your face. I looked into your eyes and saw the puppy I'd met 12 years earlier. You looked back at me and let me know we'd meet again at the Rainbow Bridge. You told me not to hurry, you'd wait patiently. The doctor turned and stepped toward us. He slowly reached for your front leg and injected that sweet release into your vein. The doc and his assistant then left the room. Even though it only took a minute for you to leave me, I stayed with you for another half hour. I wasn't ready to let you go.

There's never enough time to say good-bye.

GREAT IDEAS

Now THAT'S a great idea! This thought ricochets in my brain now and then. I'll think of something that hasn't been invented yet or, if it has, I don't know about it. Sometimes my fantastic ideas are way too costly to ever be implemented. Maybe they're just not practical, but fun. I'm pretty certain most of us have had a moment or two when we just KNEW we'd thought up some brilliant idea and all we need now is someone to design it, build it, patent it, and . . . finance it. Sigh. Always a few roadblocks to our genius, huh?

1. One year I spent a week in sunny Florida in February. When I departed St. Pete's airport, it was 77 degrees with clear, sunny skies. When I arrived at the Syracuse airport, the pilot announced it was 7 degrees and snowing. What the pilot didn't say was it had been snowing for three days. Heavily. I shuffled off the plane and crankily made my way to the luggage carousel. I snagged Big Red (what I named my suitcase on my Australia trip four years earlier) and headed for the exit. The pilot hadn't lied. It was nasty outside. The 7 degrees did not include Kevin Bacon. Sideways snow tapped my face like a 12-gauge full of frozen birdshot. I winced and then squinted my eyes in my best Clint Eastwood impression as I trudged through the parking garage and out into the long-term parking lot. I found my car under two feet of snow. And, of course, my snow brush was INSIDE my car. Yes, the car with the frozen doors. I tapped and hip-checked each door until I could finally get one to open. With Big Red safely loaded into the back seat, I turned the key in the ignition and heard a low and slow groan. I tried again. The groan was a little

louder and then the engine finally caught. Like an old man woken up from his afternoon nap, there was some grumbling. I left the motor running and stepped back outside with my brush. It took me all of 20 minutes to sweep the snow off my car and to scrape the ice from the windows. Finally, I was on my way for the three-hour drive home. That's the worst part of vacations, isn't it? The long drive home. I always told myself it was a small price to pay for the privilege of going south for a week during the coldest month of the year. I was grateful I could afford to travel and that usually pushed my bad mood aside. Traveling home was quiet and that's when I came up with a brilliant plan. At my job there's a 300-ton gantry crane. It's huge, and it moves on tracks much like a train. I was thinking these airports could have a movable contraption that blew warm air on the vehicles that were parked outside. Sort of like a car wash, but on a much drier and grander scale. Every time it snowed, someone could climb up into this bridge-like creation and maneuver it down the tracks that were embedded on either side of the parking lot. The operator would slowly pass over the whole parking lot, melting all the accumulated snow and ice from the parked vehicles. All you engineers out there, let's make this happen. On behalf of all weary travelers, I thank you.

2.   I'd like to see a silent treadmill invented, please. I have a treadmill (often referred to as my dreadmill) in my cellar. I like to watch movies while I'm walking nowhere, but the noise of the treadmill is annoying. I have to crank the television up if I want to hear what's going on in the movie. I'm not a big fan of noise, so this just irritates the bejeebers out of me. My treadmill is supposed to be one of the "quiet" ones. And, yes, it is quieter than the 'mills of old, but it's still loud enough that I can't hear the TV. Someone, please make a SILENT treadmill. It'll be a game changer and you'll be a multi-gazillionaire.

3.   I'm a dinosaur. I've never denied it. Once I find something I like, I stick with it, even if the rest of the world is moving on and

leaving me in its dust. I've always enjoyed music. I had a record collection when I was younger, then transitioned to cassettes. I skipped right over the 8-track tape era because I didn't own a car then; even if I had, I probably wouldn't have been able to afford an 8-track player. From cassettes, I migrated to the savvy compact discs. My CD collection ranges from Andrea Bocelli to ZZ Top. I've accumulated an eclectic collection of my most desired artists. My vehicle came with a CD player, and I have several boomboxes in my house that gladly accept these musical mini-records. Alas, the world moved on and everyone went to downloading onto their phones. I did not. And this is why I'd love it if someone would design a portable CD player that DOES NOT SKIP with every gentle step I take. I've had two walkabout CD players that were touted as "anti-skip" but . . . THEY LIED. They're only anti-skip if I'm standing still, on a flat surface, wearing a purple shirt, and Mercury is in retrograde. I guess I should have read the fine print disclaimer at the bottom of the user's manual. I want to play my CDs when I'm taking a walk. Is that too much to ask?

4. I need someone to install a mailbox-to-house suck-it-to-me tube like the banks have at their drive-through lanes. I admit I can be lazy, but I promise I'll only use this contraption in the worst of the winter months. Or when it's raining. Or if it's too hot and buggy outside. Having already gone through one hip replacement, I'm not eager to go through another one. I'm not crazy about getting a new knee, shoulder, or set of teeth for that matter. Snow and ice happen. Snowplows also happen. I realize the snowplow drivers aren't hitting mailboxes on purpose (wink-wink), but it would be terrible if on that ONE DAY Keanu Reeves decides to send me a love letter, the snowplow hits my mailbox and sends Keanu's letter off to the four winds. It would be lost forever and all because I didn't get to my mailbox in time because of the weather. So, you see, this is not only a matter of safety, it's a matter of the heart. Also, if you really love your aging parents, you'll install one of these for them. The ground is

still soft at this moment, so feel free to start construction on my suck-it-to-me tube anytime.

5. Someone needs to invent headphones that can be used in any theater to block out the talkers. (You rude people know who you are.) I've never been to a movie when there hasn't been at least one talker. I'm not referring to the person who screams as the knife plunges into the victim's back, or the loud laughter when Will Ferrell does his thing. I'm talking about the people who love to visit as if they're having afternoon tea at the club. No amount of shushing or nasty looks will stop these people from rambling on while the movie is playing. You can't fix people who are this rude. They think the world revolves around them. The only thing I can think of is to get special movie headphones that fit snugly, yet comfortably, over our ears. The only sound we'd hear is what's coming from the movie. An added bonus: if you have long hair, these headphones will hold it back, so you don't accidentally sweep your buttered popcorn with your tresses.

6. I wish big bags of flour and sugar came in sturdy plastic reusable containers. Hear me out on this one. I was in the grocery store with my mother one time, and she asked me to pick up a bag of sugar. It was the 20-lb. bag, of course. I placed it into the cart, and I must have accidentally pressed it against a sharp corner of a box. Little did either of us realize, that corner had poked a small hole in the bag of sugar. We meandered up and down several aisles picking out items and placing them in our cart. My mother looked at her list, said she'd forgotten to pick up spaghetti, and asked me to go back two aisles to grab it. I turned to retrace our steps and that's when I saw the sugar on the floor. There was a small stream, then a pile. Then another stream, another pile. Obviously, the piles happened when we had stopped to look at something, then moved along to create the sugar stream. I started laughing and went back to my mother and our cart. I leaned the then slightly lighter bag of sugar on its side and saw the hole. We started giggling. I pointed out our

sugar trail and Ma just shook her head. We finished our shopping and headed straight to the service desk to confess our sin. The manager gave us a knowing smile and said it wasn't a problem. He assured us that wasn't the first time, and it wouldn't be the last that had happened. (Thank you, Richard of Sun Foods.) It was an accident and accidents happen. Richard called for a cleanup on aisle five. And four. And three. He hustled back to the baking section and picked up another bag of sugar and brought it to the front of the store where we were. My mother said she'd pay for both bags, but the manager just laughed and changed the lighter bag for the full one and sent us on our way. So why don't they sell big sacks in Rubbermaid-type containers? I'd even settle for super-durable, flexible nylon bags. Cost. It's all about cost. I know I can't be the only person out there who wouldn't mind paying a little extra to NOT leave a trail.

7. We're never going to stop cigarette production or usage. We're never going to stop smokers from carelessly tossing their butts onto the ground. How about inventing a quickly dissolving filter? Once the cigarette is lit, the filter only lasts, say, ten minutes. Then it self-destructs like something out of a *Mission Impossible* movie. Maybe there can be some way to load the filter with a potion that once it gets so much smoke drawn through it, it crumbles into ashes itself. No more stepping on nasty cigarette butts.

8. Rechargeable battery-operated back scratchers that can be affixed to a door frame. Think about it. No more reaching with sticks, spatulas, or rulers. No more begging your spouse to scratch an itch you can't reach. I've always loved having my back scratched, but for some reason never found a partner willing to give me two minutes of pleasure. (Read into THAT what you will.) I even went as far as to buy a small soft bristle hairbrush for a boyfriend to use on my back because he said he didn't like the idea of getting skin under his fingernails. Gee, I didn't ask him to claw me! But he wouldn't even use the brush because it

wasn't beneficial to him, so why should he even bother? Here's my idea: this contraption would be about the size of your palm. It would have different bristle attachments. If you like a softer touch, go for the light bristles. Do you enjoy a good scraping? Attach the heavy-duty brush. This gizmo would snap onto any open door frame, beam, or post. All you'd have to do is turn the power on and stand in front of it as a small arm reaches out and slowly, lovingly scratches you up and down, side to side, and in circles. Pure bliss. Once the inventor has this model perfected, he/she can make a waterproof one for scrubbing in the shower. I'm willing to back this endeavor financially, so reach out to me, you creative minds.

9. I'm still on a quest to find long winter socks that stay up and don't bunch up in the arch of my foot. I'm sure they've been invented already and probably cost $50 per pair, but I need someone to invent affordable ones. Every time I wear my heavy boots, my socks get tired and slink down my calves and ankles, resting in a wad in the middle of my sole. I've tried the compression socks that cling to my calves like a spoiled toddler clings to its mother. They stay up but are so uncomfortable. Oh sure, I'm spoiled with wanting to feel my lower leg and foot area. What's a little numbness in exchange for socks that stay up? When I go out snowshoeing, I wear my comfy, warm boots. No matter what kind of socks I wear, they always end up filling my foot gap. I'm not about to wear sock garters, and cuddly tights won't work because I don't want all that bulk on my upper legs and derriere area. Short of a staple gun, I've pretty much run out of ideas. Help me?

10. I need a special oven to compensate for my short attention span. I'm not a trained baker and never professed to be one. I do like to dabble in my kitchen from time to time. With the price of baking ingredients climbing every week, it's more important than ever to NOT waste anything. I sometimes use my stove's timer, but not often. Or maybe I'll hear the DING and think,

okay, I have time to do this one more thing before I have to take the goodies out of the oven. Then I chide myself for every batch of cookies I leave in the oven a few minutes too long. Okay, so they're edible, but only if I dunk them in hot coffee for a minute. I'm looking for an oven I can program to automatically sense when my cookies are done, put the oven temperature on pause, and to open the door and lift the cookie sheet out and rest it on top. Of course, the lifting device will fold back into the waiting oven. This way, when I'm distracted with other chores or a phone call, my cookies (or cinnamon rolls, breads, cupcakes, whatever) won't overbake or burn. You're probably thinking this is the height of laziness or inattentiveness. And you wouldn't be wrong. I do have a timer on my oven so I can set it to shut off after a specified number of minutes, but that means whatever's inside will still be in the residual heat, drying out and getting crusty. I need that lifter-outer!

11. Does anyone have a self-cleaning lint filter on their dryer? Imagine being able to push the "START" button to dry your clothes but first there's a little chime indicating the machine is sucking out all that lint and depositing it directly into a tiny receptacle on the side, much like a gumball machine. This brilliant machine mixes the lint with a fine mist of water, then rolls it into a small ball so you don't get all that dryer lint dust on your hands, sink, floor, or anywhere else you may come near with it. These little wads of slightly damp dryer lint are easily disposed of without the mess.

I could probably go on with a few more, but I don't want to give away all my bright ideas. The patent office is calling, so I'll stop right here.

CHANGE IS GOOD

    As I get older, I seem to appreciate the smaller things in life more than ever. At times I'm like a wide-eyed child, seeing things for the first time. Other times, it finally hits me that I've taken certain moments for granted and I should be more aware. Some people need constant input, noise, entertainment, or anything to take them out of the present. I know people who are afraid to be alone with their thoughts. They crave commotion every waking minute. Why? What is it about their own mind, their own thoughts, that scares them so much? As I mentally flip the pages on my life's calendar, I've become more introspective. I cherish the silence of an early morning. Sitting on my porch late at night and staring at the stars is divine. Sometimes it's in these quiet moments that we hear the most. Just last night I was sitting outside enjoying the stillness around me. I thought about the current situation down south where yet another hurricane has hit and displaced so many people. Then there was the news about the fires out west. Too damned dry, and everything is like kindling, going up in smoke in seconds. That's when I realized just how much I enjoy and appreciate where I live. I admit the thought of going south for the harshest part of winter entices me now and then, but I just can't seem to pull that trigger yet. I have plenty of friends who are either snowbirds or they've moved south permanently. Without fail, they all say the same thing: I miss October in New York. Then they add in how they also miss the change of seasons we have up here. They don't miss it enough to move back, but that's the trade-off you get when you move to a warmer clime. I'm one of those people who enjoys the changing seasons. All of our seasons have something special to offer, and I'd feel cheated if I didn't experience each one as the months marched on every year.

Let's begin with spring. Ah, that eternal fresh start. People seem to come out of hibernation in the spring. By the end of March, those of us in the upper regions of our country are ready for a break. We anticipate mud season with quiet glee. It'll be brown, gray, and messy, but what follows is delightful! The first tufts of green grass start reaching up through last year's fallen blades. Trees will be budding out with their tiny leaves unfurling like millions of Arbor Day flags. The air becomes sweeter as the snow melts and streams begin to trickle again. Our ears perk up as we hear the birds chirping as if to welcome spring with their songs. I pull out my hummingbird feeders and within days my little buddies are back, ready to zoom around my head as I sit on my deck sipping morning coffee or evening cocktails. My mind drifts to this new season's potential. Which flowers will I plant in the front garden? Will I take on any new projects that will make my home more comfy or spiffy? Is my lawnmower all set for more laps than the Indy 500? Do I have enough twine for my trimmer? I relish the lack of worry I'm afforded at this point in my life. The only thing I'm not crazy about at springtime is the bugs. If you've ever seen what I look like after a black fly bites me, you understand. Once again, I'm reminded of how the universe likes to prove balance in everything. Fresh grass? YES! Bugs? NO! The good and the bad. Yin and yang.

Moving on to summer, my smile gets even wider as I see those flowers I planted in the spring pop up and bloom. The colors are vibrant and almost yell at me, "HEY! CHECK THIS OUT!" I thoroughly enjoy the botanical palette that adorns the front of my home. I feel almost virtuous as the honeybees flit from one bloom to the next, gathering pollen and nectar. The blazing sun and high humidity remind me to appreciate my friend and classmate, Terry Goodrich. He's the angel who installed my central air conditioning and every year at the peak of summer, I send a thank you to Terry and his crew. If I'd known I was going to appreciate air conditioning THIS much, I would have had him install it much sooner. Summer also brings the intoxicating smell of freshly cut hay. Several neighbors are farmers, and the haying season is busy every year. The chatter of tractors, balers, and wagons on the road sends me back in time to when I was a kid tossing bales on the family farm. I give a knowing nod when I see my friends heading toward their barns with wagons loaded with sustenance for the cows this winter. The mid-year months mean gardens are producing and generous friends will leave just-picked vegetables on your porch, another reminder of how beautiful and bountiful country living in the summertime can be. The simplicity of rural life, especially in the summer, is satisfying to the soul. As I said, it's the little things I'm noticing now, and it makes me chuckle when I realize how much I've taken for granted.

At this very moment, I'm looking out my living room window and smiling. It's October and the leaves are on fire. Figuratively, that is. They're ablaze in colors that defy description. Merely saying they're yellow and red seems to do them a terrible injustice. How grateful I am for my eyesight! I've been on this big blue marble for almost sixty-one years now, and nature never fails to humble me. I'm in constant awe of her beauty and surprises. Sometimes nature scares me. She can be cruel on a whim. She can be delightful when she wants but just make sure you never underestimate her. Fall is my favorite time of year and, if those random surveys are accurate at all, I'm not alone with my preference. The air is crisp. The smell of fallen leaves wafts up to your nose as you walk on them and hear their crunch. For a moment I'm sad, thinking it's almost time to hunker down for another long winter, but then I snap myself out of it. I greedily soak up every minute of autumn that I can. I'm outside more at this time of year than any other. Between the gorgeous sight of the leaves exploding into their own fireworks displays, to the scent of apples and pumpkins everywhere, October can't be beat. If I could trade one month of winter for another month of fall, I'd be in heaven.

Not to say winter is bad, mind you. Many years ago when I was still working I ran into a retired former co-worker. It was mid-February, minus thirty degrees, and sideways snow was blowing about the parking lot as we walked into the grocery store at the same time. Once we were inside, I looked at him and asked, "Why the HELL aren't you in Florida?" He laughed and said yes, he does have a place down there, had been south a couple of times this winter, and would go again soon.

Then he let me in on a little secret, "Winters don't suck once you're retired. Seriously, I like the changing seasons up here and I prefer the slower pace of Brasher. When I check the forecast and see we have a winter storm coming in, I'll hit the store and make sure I have enough food and beer. I'll swing by the library and check out a pile of books. Sometimes I'll hit the lumberyard and pick up some wood for a few projects I've been thinking about lately. Then I hunker down in my house or heated garage, and just ride out the storm with a smile on my face. There's a difference between HAVING to get out in the cold and snow (when you're working) and CHOOSING to go out in it (when you're retired)."

I laughed. I was still five years away from retirement and this mindset was foreign to me. Still, his words sunk into my head. And I'll be damned, he was right. I've been retired almost six years and I haven't dreaded winter ONCE. Not once. I've followed in my co-worker's footsteps every winter since I punched out for the last time. There are days when I stand in front of my picture window, sip my coffee or tea, and shake my head. NOPE. Not going out today. I laugh, grab a book, and plant my hinder-ender in my big comfy leather chair. Or maybe I'll bake. I'll possibly watch television or maybe write a story or two. Then the sunny days pop up and I break out my snowshoes and head out to OK Acres for a tromp in the woods. Thanks to Tom Storrin, I can hike on perfectly groomed trails and then go into his camp and warm up if I've gotten too chilly on my trek. Winter won't keep me inside for months on end. There's too much to enjoy out there, even when it's freezing. On a positive note, there aren't any bugs biting me while I'm snowshoeing, so I count that as a WIN for winter.

And that brings us back around to spring again. I can see some of you nodding your heads already. You agree with me, or maybe partially. The revolving seasons up here are breathtaking and give us so much to appreciate. I don't think I'd be as happy in a year-round 90-degree abode. I'd become dismayed or complacent. I'd get cranky. And I think we can all agree the last thing we need is more crankiness in this world. I'll stick with my four seasons and if I reach a point where I need a change, I can book a flight to almost anywhere and go. Maybe in this case I CAN have it all.

ETERNALLY YOURS

"I'll see you again soon." Those were the words Milton always said when I was getting ready to leave. It was his way of inviting me back again without sounding too needy or demanding. Being old and lonely is hard on anyone, but especially for those without a spouse or children. Too many widows and widowers out there are just getting along day by day. They don't ask for much but have so much to give in return.

I met Milt in our local library. He and I were both perusing the latest whodunit books, and we struck up a conversation. We compared favorite authors, characters, plot twists, and by the end of our hour-long visit, I was convinced I'd just met my elderly male self. He told me he lived close by in the senior's complex and he walked to the library on most days when the weather was good. Milt made a point of letting me know exactly what his schedule was, so I was pretty sure he was telling me if I ever wanted to visit with him again, I could find him there at the library between those particular hours.

Milton was born in 1928 to a farm family near Buffalo, NY. He and his two sisters worked with their parents on a small dairy farm that had been passed down from Milt's grandparents. The plan was for Milt to take over when his parents were old enough to call it quits. The two sisters begrudgingly worked on the farm but living the big city life in Buffalo was more to their taste, so they were happy to sign the farm over to their big brother when the time came.

Over the next year or so, anytime I wanted to stop in at the library, I made a point of going between 11:00 a.m. and 2:00

p.m. It was a rare occasion that I didn't find him there at his designated time. I'd go in and wander around until I ran into him, then we'd sit in a corner and quietly chat for a while. He had plenty of stories to tell and advice to give. To say I enjoyed his company would be a gross understatement.

"Did I ever tell you about the first time I laid eyes on Clara?" Milt had asked me this same question at least twice before, but my reply was always the same.

"I can't remember if you did or not, Milt. Can you tell me again?" And then he'd launch into his love story with Clara.

"I got drafted into the Army back in '51. That's when the Korean conflict happened. I never understood why they called it a conflict when people were fighting and dying. Isn't that war? In my eyes it was." Milt's eyes squinted in the bright sunlight beaming through the front windows of the library. I could tell he was remembering the events of 1951 as clearly as if they'd just happened yesterday.

"I'm a big guy. I'm kinda hard to miss." He stretched his long corduroy-covered legs out in front of him as if to prove a point. "Back then I was six-foot-five. Now I've shrunk down to about six-foot-two or so. I don't think the Knicks will be calling me anytime soon," he chuckled. "I weighed about two-and-a-half, but it was all solid muscle. I grew up on a farm and we didn't have all that fancy equipment they have now. I swear farmers are gonna get lazy with kicker balers and hay elevators in their haymows and such!" His head shook side to side.

Milt was still an imposing figure at six-foot-two, and I'd guess about 200 pounds, maybe a few more. He held it well, no pot belly and no slouching humpback. Just broad shoulders and long limbs. I grinned at the thought of a young, strapping Milt tossing hay, a bale in each hand, up into the high haymow of a barn.

"So, I got drafted. Did my basic training and was stationed at Ft. Dix in New Jersey. I was allowed to go on leave just before I had to ship out to Korea, so I took the bus home to Buffalo. Maybe that's where that song came from . . . 'Shuffle off to Buffalo!'" He slapped his knee and hummed a few bars from the song. "I spent about a week with my family, then I had to get back on that bus and head east. I knew it was going to be a long ride, and I had time to kill, so I ducked into a little diner not far from the bus stop." Milt scratched his stubbly-bearded chin as his eyes started to sparkle. I knew this story by heart but never tired hearing it.

"In order to get a cheap bus fare, I had to be in uniform. I was all decked out and was carrying my duffel bag. I dropped my bag into the third booth on the right and just as I was taking my hat off, the prettiest girl in the world came over with a menu." Milt's face went completely mushy. All of his wrinkles softened, his eyes shone, and a wide grin stretched across the real estate under his nose. "I was a goner. Yes sir. I don't know the exact minute, but it was somewhere between 11:00 and 12:00. How do I know that, you ask? I know because I had to be at the bus stop at noon to catch my bus and I knew I had only one hour to grab a bite before my long ride back to Jersey. I sat down and ordered coffee. I could barely get the words out of my mouth, that's how smitten I was."

"You must have been quite striking, all six and a half feet of you, decked out in your uniform and all." I gave him a wink and a slight nudge with my elbow.

"I've never been stuck on myself, but yeah, I guess the uniform helped. Even a farm boy like me can look good all gussied up like that!"

I nodded and waited for more.

"She brought my coffee, and I noticed her name tag read 'Clara' and for some reason it stuck in my head. She was a little shy but smiled at me and I swear the whole diner lit up when she did. I ordered the hot roast beef sandwich with gravy and mashed potatoes. When she brought it to my table, I was shocked at how much was on my plate. I was really hungry, so I gave her a grin and told her how glad I was that the cook wasn't stingy with the portions." At this point he patted his stomach and smacked his lips as if he was eating that lunch all over again. "Clara looked at me and said something about how it takes a lot of food to fill up a big guy. I agreed and told her I definitely had a good appetite. We chatted a little longer, then she went off to wait on more tables. Every now and then she'd come back over and refill my coffee cup and give me another shy smile. I loved it."

"But then you had to catch a bus, right?"

"Yup. I caught that bus. And I went back to the base. A few days later I was on my way to Korea. The whole time I was traveling, all I could think of was Clara, that pretty little brown-haired gal in the diner. She reminded me of Audrey Hepburn. Cute, but spunky."

"It's too bad you didn't have more time to get to know each other back then."

"Oh, don't you worry. God had a plan for us. I couldn't get her off my mind. One day when I had some down time, I wrote her a letter. Mind you, I had no idea what her last name was. I addressed the envelope to just Clara, and the name of the restaurant. I didn't even have the street number of the restaurant, just the street name. I reminded her of who I was and said it was okay if she didn't remember me. I was polite and thanked her for being so kind to me just before I shipped out. I said a little prayer and put my letter in the outgoing mail pouch."

My heart was getting all soft and squishy. I knew where this was going and wanted to hear it again.

"It was a little over a month later that I received a letter back. SHE WROTE BACK! You have no idea how much mail means to guys overseas. Seeing my name written in her pretty handwriting on that envelope nearly gave me a heart attack. I wanted to tear it open, but I didn't want to ruin it. I took my jackknife out and carefully opened it. I slid two pages out of the pink envelope and read the letter that would change my life."

Looking over at Milt I noticed his eyes watering a little bit. He blinked a few times then went on with his story.

"She wrote she remembered me. Clara told me about her job and how busy she'd been but getting a letter back to me was a priority. Clara told me a little bit about her family, mentioned the weather, and then closed with a request for me to be careful and come back soon."

Milt's chest heaved with a huge sigh.

"I knew right then and there that Clara was going to be my wife someday. Don't ask me how I knew just from one letter, but I did. I swear. As God is my witness, I knew." Milt raised his right hand toward the heavens. I just smiled and said I believed him.

"We exchanged letters for over a year. Mail was slower back then. Still, every single one of those letters was precious to me. And to her, too. I came home alive and kicking but it was another six months before my enlistment was up and I could go home. I made it back to Buffalo and the diner was the first place I stopped. When I walked in, she was waiting on a table but had her back to me. I just stood there. She finally turned around and saw me. Now, remember, back then ladies were ladies and gentlemen were gentlemen. She walked sort of fast toward me. I met her halfway. It was just like those sappy movies. I held my hands out to her and instead of putting her hands in mine . . . she flung herself against my chest. What could I do? I wrapped my arms around her and lifted her up in a bear hug! Everyone in the diner was clapping. (I found out later she'd told her co-workers and regulars at the diner about me.) Am I getting too long-winded here?"

"No, you're just fine. I want to hear every detail, Milt."

"Well, I'll try to shorten it a little for you. Needless to say, we were married soon after. I ended up taking over the family farm. My folks let us set up a little trailer on the property so that worked out great. Eventually, they passed, and we moved into the main house. We weren't blessed with any children, but we still had a wonderful, happy, fulfilling life together."

I reached over and grabbed his hand and gave it a squeeze.

"I still have all of our letters. They're all together in a box in my dresser now."

I could just imagine Milt reading and re-reading their letters on rainy days. They never had children, so these letters were all he had left of Clara. Ah, the power of the written word.

I love a good love story and every time Milt told me this one, I loved it even more.

One day I ran into Milt at the library, and he looked a bit smaller. I asked him how he was doing and that's when he gave me the news. He had pancreatic cancer. I choked. I knew this was a fast-acting cancer and survival rates were extremely low. At his age, his chance of survival was almost zero. He rallied and said for me not to worry because he'd had a long and happy life. And soon he'd be with Clara again. I started bawling. He was comforting me over his impending death. How selfish was I?

"I have a favor to ask of you," Milt softly said.

"Anything."

"Meet me here tomorrow around noon, okay? We'll talk about it then."

"I'll be here."

The next day I showed up just before noon. Milt was already at a table in the corner. He waved me over to him. On the table was a large shoe box. He opened the box and showed me all of the letters he and Clara had exchanged over the years. He pulled his first letter out and showed me the envelope. Sure enough, it was addressed to just Clara at the restaurant in Buffalo. I laughed right out loud. Then he showed me her first letter and asked me to read it. It was exactly as he'd relayed it to me earlier.

"I have a favor to ask of you. You can say no if you want, but it would mean the world to me, and probably to Clara, if you'd do it. No pressure." I love it when people say "no pressure" because it's exactly what they're doing!

"I'll do it as long as it doesn't involve me wearing an orange prison jumpsuit," I said this with a cocky smirk on my face.

"I can't make any promises about THAT," he said. "What I'd like is after I go, would you read these letters? I've told you so much about Clara and our life together, but I want to share what we had with you. I think you're the kind of person who could appreciate the sentiment in them."

I nodded. The lump in my throat wouldn't let me reply.

"Once you're done reading them, I'd like you to bring them to the cemetery where Clara and I are buried side-by-side. I want you to bury them right smack-dab in the middle of us. These are OUR letters, not just mine. I can't hoard them and keep them in my casket for all eternity. That wouldn't be fair. So, if you could just dig a little hole and put our letters right in the middle of us, I'd appreciate that with all my heart."

The vision of an orange jumpsuit slithered through my mind. It wasn't grave robbing. Not if I'm *adding* to a grave, right? But it would still be digging a hole, and maybe a bit more than to just plant pansies. Oh boy. How was I going to do this without getting caught? Or hauled away to the nuthouse?

"I'll do it. No problem. Easy peasy, Milt! And if I don't, you have permission to haunt the hell out of me!"

"Hey, kid, I plan to do that if I can anyway, so you lose!"

We laughed and visited just as normally as we could, considering the circumstances. About two hours later I got up, hugged him softly, and gave him a peck on his withered cheek. I thanked him for his friendship and his faith in me. I told him I was honored to hold his letters and to place them where they belong when the time came. He hugged me back and gave me a peck on the top of my head. He said he knew he had the right person for the job. I walked away and looked back once to wave good-bye. I knew it was the last time I'd see Milt alive.

Less than a month later I saw his obituary in the newspaper. There were no calling hours, just a quick burial next to Clara. The night of his burial, I opened the shoe box and started reading his treasured letters. He'd arranged them in chronological order. It was as if I was sitting in a room watching and listening to the two of them talking about their lives. One in Buffalo, one in Korea, then later in New Jersey. In one envelope that wasn't addressed to either of them was an old diner receipt. Clara had kept the slip she'd taken Milt's order on all those years ago. It clearly showed roast beef dinner, extra. Meaning extra portions on one plate. And the time was written in the corner so the cook would know which order he had to cook next. The time she wrote? 11:11. Now, I don't know how many of you are superstitious, but I certainly am. It's been said the time to pray for what you want and the time the angels can hear you is 11:11. Interesting.

It took me two weeks to read all of their letters. I didn't get too greedy and read them all at once. I rationed them so I could appreciate them more. The love and patience they showed in those letters reminded me of how life should be and how I need to work on my impatient attitude.

When I was done reading all of the letters, I placed them in a vacuum-seal food bag and sealed them. I put that bag into another one and vacuumed that one too. Then, one bright Monday morning I went to the cemetery. I took a bucket with a few small pots of flowers in it. I took my sharp hand spade and an old blanket with me. I parked my car as closely to their plot as possible, laid out my blanket as if I was using it to protect my knees while planting the flowers. I probably looked like a gopher, popping my head up every minute or so to see if anyone was watching me. The ground between the two graves wasn't very wide, and lucky for me, it was soft enough that my hand spade could dig deep enough to bury the letters. I dug about eighteen inches down and placed the letters in the hole. I filled in the hole, tamped it down, and replaced the grassy sod on top. You could barely tell anything had been disturbed at all. I planted the flowers on either side of the stones and said my final good-bye.

I kept my promise.

FOLLOW UPS

I've had a few requests for follow ups on some of my stories in *Brain Scraps*, so here you go!

1. Yes, I do still eat pepperoni. And, of course, I still smile and say hello to my mother as I'm buying it and as I'm getting ready to cut it up. I HAVE to buy the stick, not the pre-sliced ones. If you know, you know.

2. No, I have not taught any youngsters that bag of corn by the side of the road trick. For some reason my friends don't want me teaching their impressionable children these "Oscar" jokes.

3. I'm still having those very real dreams that I'm speaking in another language, but I haven't yet figured out what it is. I only WISH it was Italian! Reincarnation still interests me.

4. NOOOOO! I have NOT taken any "toys" in my carry-on luggage again! But if I did, I'd make sure there were no batteries installed.

5. Yes, I've taken several people to that back field where Jerry might be resting. A few friends are very sensitive, and they swear they can "feel" something under that big tree, near that stone.

6. I haven't even attempted to donate blood. I realize it was many years ago the Red Cross asked me not to bother anymore, but I still haven't mustered up the courage to try to give them my precious AB+ again. Maybe 2023 will be my lucky year.

7. Now and then I'll pick up a big sack of flour when I'm at

BJ's and I ALWAYS take extra care when lifting. Because . . . you know . . . I don't want to lose any girly parts.

8.   Thankfully, I have not had another birthday as bad as my 42nd, and hope I never do. I've had a few disappointing birthdays since that one, but I still haven't given up hope.

9. I still haven't developed a taste for cabbage rolls, but my face lights up and I laugh when I see the sign at the local church advertising their cabbage roll suppers.

10. Yes, I'm still superstitious and trying some of those ideas from the older folks. I've had a few good things happen to me or have been given an item right out of the blue, so maybe those good luck charms are working.

11.   I don't need to go midnight gardening anymore. My generous neighbors make sure I don't have to resort to a life of crime.

12. Danielle is still in her interesting home, and although it's not as spiritually active as it was a few years ago, she's still reminded she has roommates. She's not freaked out or scared anymore, so that's a good thing.

13. I've been doing pretty well with writing letters and mailing them. I still get texts or emails letting me know how much it means to certain people when they can hold such a personal touch as a handwritten letter.

14. I haven't been doing much Barn Ninja-ing lately, but maybe I'll get back to it during the cooler weather. I know the recipients of my labor will always welcome me with open arms.

15. My thoughts about my final hour are pretty much the same. I'll have to wait and see if I'm in the mood for coffee or if maybe it's a shot of peanut butter whiskey that'll be next to me.

ACKNOWLEDGEMENTS

This is the part where I wear out the phrase "thank you." It's not easy to thank everyone who has had your back, but I'll try to name a few.

First and foremost, there's the lovely Lisa Winters who fixes everything. Without her time and talent, I'd be floundering and my mistakes would glare at you from every page. Thank you, Lisa, for all you do.

To my faithful guinea pigs Alicia Mere and Roger LaShomb, thank you for letting me run these stories by you and for giving me honest feedback. I love how you never pull any punches.

I can't give enough thanks to Alisa Lobdell for her constant support and encouragement in everything I do, or attempt to do. Alisa has been my sounding board for every part of my life for over 30 years. Alisa, I'm grateful to you for our friendship and because you'll never tell where the bodies are buried.

Thank you doesn't seem to be enough for the posse. For Katy Collette, Michelle Gauthier, Susan Ryan, Debbie Pitts, Norine Hull, Marcy Smutz, Ruthie Sanford, Sici Kahrs, Shari Gilman, Kate Hey, Joanne LaBarge, and Ceci Roy, these two little words aren't enough for all the support you've shown me over the years. But I'll say them again anyway. Thank you.

My heart will never be as big as Diane Kennedy's but I'm okay with that. Thank you, Diane, for your generosity, kindness, smiles, and love. You truly are a gem in my crown of friends.

As much as it pains me, I have to say thank you to my cousin David L. Thomas. Yeah, yeah, yeah, okay. I said it. Are you happy now, Dave? All kidding aside, Dave has been nothing but a cheerleader and always happy for me when I accomplish anything. You're a good guy, Dave. Thank you.

My gratitude also goes out to Dr. Nancy Frost and Dr. Donna Mosier for their uplifting encouragement and attagirl attitude. You ladies have never had any doubts about me and I appreciate that more than you know.

To Tom Storrin, I give you my most sincere thanks for your friendship and utmost confidence in me. Entrusting me to dogsit Durk is an honor. Also, I appreciate you for taking such good care of OK Acres. That piece of heaven is in good hands.

My gratitude goes to Kevin Crinklaw for sharing his beloved pups Canon and Bart with me. There's nothing better than the love of a good dog, and these two hold a special place in my heart. Adirondac Bart, I'll see your smiling face again someday.

I write about being grateful for the little things in life, and that includes being appreciative of where I live. I have the best neighbors who keep an eye out for me, supply me with goodies from their gardens, and always have the best advice. Thanks for looking out for me, Gary and Roxy Munson, Pat McKeown, and Karen St. Hilaire. I certainly won the neighbor lottery when I moved here.

To Gary A. and Richard M., I give you two guys a huge nod for being there for me through thick and thin. You understand me more than you'll ever realize. You've helped me see through different eyes, and always with much clearer vision. Thank you.

To all of you who have given me the thumbs-up, smiles, and have thanked me for sharing my stories, I am truly humbled and will always be grateful. Your kindness and generosity mean so much to me. Thank you.

ABOUT THE AUTHOR

Pendra J. King

Pendra J. King was born into a large family and grew up on a small dairy farm in northern New York. She learned early on that everyone has a story to tell. Some people have several stories and, if you sit quietly and listen, you may learn something. An aspiring author since childhood, she always knew a book or two would be in her future. Gathering these stories and putting them together for others to enjoy has been a dream come true for her. Sharing intimate moments of her life is her way of letting people know they're not alone. We all go through ups and downs, and how we deal with them speaks volumes. King prefers to see the humor in most circumstances because, as she says, she'd rather laugh than cry. At this very moment she's plodding through her notebooks to see if there's enough for volume #3 of Brain Scraps.

BOOKS BY THIS AUTHOR

Brain Scraps

Brain Scraps is a collection of personal stories and essays of experiences, interviews, and observances that offer a variety of feelings and emotions for the reader. Love, hope, and happiness abound within these pages. Fear, anger, and resolve pop up now and then. The reader will go from laughing out loud to sitting quietly with a lump in their throat with Brain Scraps.

Made in the USA
Las Vegas, NV
28 December 2022

64287502R00118